Europe's Elected Parliament

Contemporary European Studies, 5

Series Editor
Clive Archer

Co-Editor
Judy Batt

Europe's Elected Parliament

Julie Smith

Sheffield
Academic Press

Copyright © 1999 Sheffield Academic Press

Published by
Sheffield Academic Press Ltd
Mansion House
19 Kingfield Road
Sheffield S11 9AS
England

Typeset by Sheffield Academic Press
and
Printed on acid-free paper in Great Britain
by Cromwell Press
Trowbridge, Wiltshire

British Library Cataloguing in Publication Data

A catalogue record for this book is available
from the British Library

ISBN 1-85075-999-5

Contents

Figures

Tables

Series Foreword

Contemporary European Studies is now in its second year of publication. It represents a continuing collaboration between the University Association for Contemporary European Studies (UACES) and Sheffield Academic Press.

In 2000 UACES will celebrate 30 years of being the foremost organization that brings together academics and practitioners from disciplines concerned with the study of contemporary Europe in the United Kingdom. In the lead up to this anniversary, the Association initiated the Contemporary European Studies series to respond to the needs of those studying and teaching about contemporary Europe, with special emphasis on the institutions and policies of the European Union. As series editor, I wish to ensure that the four publications during 1999 cover issues of relevance and interest in what may well prove to be a crucial year for the European Union.

It is therefore fitting that 'Europe's elected parliament' should be the subject of the first volume in 1999, the year that sees the direct election of Members of the European Parliament from the now fifteen EU Member States. Julie Smith, a fellow of Robinson College, Cambridge, has both taught and researched this subject. Her book assesses the present European Parliament against the expectations and fears surrounding the introduction of direct elections 20 years ago. She examines the record of the new elections since then, looking at the European-level political parties, the campaigns, and the election turnout and results. She provides an informed and balanced view of the contribution that the new Members of the European Parliament may make to democracy within the EU.

I am grateful to Jean Allen, Rebecca Cullen and the staff at Sheffield Academic Press for their assistance in the production of this volume, and to Geoffrey Edwards of the Centre of International Studies, Cambridge University, for his guidance.

Clive Archer
Series Editor

Acknowledgments

This book began as a doctoral thesis, albeit in a rather different form. I therefore owe a debt of gratitude to many people. While it is somewhat invidious to single out individuals, a few people have been particularly helpful over the last few years and deserve a special mention.

Thanks are due to the Economic and Social Reseach Council for funding my doctoral research. I am also very grateful for grants from the Raymond Carr Fund and the Committee for Graduate Studies of the University of Oxford, and for a Sørensen Award for travel and research expenses from the European Communities Archives.

I am enormously grateful to all the Members of the European Parliament and officials in the Parliament, Commission, parties and party groups who gave so freely of their time to fill in the gaps in my knowledge. In particular, I would mention Timothy Bainbridge, Martyn Bond, Ken Collins MEP, Richard Corbett MEP, Francis Jacobs, David Martin MEP, Michael Shackleton, James Spence, Anthony Teasdale, Graham Watson MEP and Martin Westlake.

I have benefited greatly from academic guidance from several people. Roger Morgan kindly commented on the first draft of the thesis. Without the statistical help of Anthony Heath, several chapters would have been much the poorer. My DPhil supervisor, William Wallace, gave very considerable support and guidance. The comments of my thesis examiners, David Butler and Martin Westlake, were also very helpful. I could not have transformed the thesis into this form without the efforts and thought-provoking comments of Clive Archer and Geoffrey Edwards.

I am also indebted to Charlotte Lindberg Clausen and Christopher Kirwan for research and editorial help, without which the book might never have materialized, to Rachael Taft for help with the Index, and to Rebecca Cullen at Sheffield Academic Press for all her work on the production side. As always, responsibility for any errors rests with me.

Julie Smith
Cambridge, April 1999

Abbreviations

CDS	Centre Social Democrats (Portugal)
CDU	Christian Democratic Union (Germany)
CFSP	Common Foreign and Security Policy
CSP	Confederation of the Socialist Parties of the EC
CSU	Christian Social Union (Germany)
D'66	Democracy 66 (Netherlands)
EC	European Communities
ECOSOC	Economic and Social Committee of the EU
ECJ	European Court of Justice
ECSC	European Coal and Steel Community
EDA	Group of the European Democratic Alliance
EDC	European Defence Community
EDG	European Democratic Group
EEC	European Economic Community
ELDR	Federation of European Liberals, Democrats and Reformers/European Liberal Democrat and Reform Party
EN	Europe of Nations Group
EP	European Parliament
EPP	European People's Party
ERA	Group of the European Radical Alliance
EU	European Union
EUL/NGL	The Confederal Group of the European United Left/Nordic Green Left
Euratom	European Atomic Energy Community
FDP	Free Democrat Party (Germany)
FE	*Forza Europa* Group
FN	National Front (France)
FOE	first order election
GREENS	Group of the Greens in the EP
IGC	Intergovernmental Conference
I-EN	Group of Independents for a Europe of Nations
JHA	Justice and Home Affairs
MEP	Member of the European Parliament
N-A	Non-attached MEPs

PDS	Party of Democratic Socialism (Germany)
	Party of the Democratic Left (Italy)
PES	Party of European Socialists
PP	Popular Party (Spain)
PR	proportional representation
PSD	Portuguese Social Democratic Party
QMV	qualified majority voting
RPR	Rally for the Republic (French Gaullists)
SEA	Single European Act
SOE	second order election
SPD	Social Democratic Party (Germany)
TEU	Treaty on European Union (Maastricht Treaty)
UDF	Union for French Democracy
UFE	Union for Europe
VVD	Liberal Party (Netherlands)
WEU	West European Union

1 |

Introduction

Either Europe will be democratic or there will be no such thing as Europe.[1]

The twentieth anniversary of the first direct elections to the European Parliament (EP) will be marked in 1999. 1999 also sees the expansion of the EP's powers resulting from the 1997 Treaty of Amsterdam, just in time for the fifth set of EP elections.[2] The first four sets of European elections were generally characterized by low voter turnout and limited participation by major politicians; with the exception of Denmark, the campaigns and results were determined by national issues and led by national political parties. European elections are often considered to be 'second-order', similar to local rather than national elections in nature and significance. Yet this approach ignores certain more fundamental questions: Why is there a directly-elected European Parliament? Should we expect European elections to resemble national elections? What lessons do European elections offer for an understanding of transnational democracy? The aim of this book is to analyse the hopes and fears of those 'present at the creation' and demonstrate how far the experience of direct elections has met their expectations.

The European Parliament is part of a unique experiment in regional integration. The European Union (EU) differs from traditional patterns of international organizations in having a far more developed and autonomous set of institutions. For many of the founders, including Robert Schuman, whose plan outlining proposals for the creation of a European Coal and Steel Community (ECSC) marked the start of formal European integration, the aim was inherently political. Thus the institutions created, including the Parliament, could in many ways be seen as analogous to those in nation states.

1. Headline in French newspaper, after remarks made by President of the European Commission, Jacques Delors, cited by the then President of the European Parliament, Egon Klepsch (1992: 7).

2. The Treaty of Amsterdam, signed in October 1997, should have come into effect by June 1999.

The nature of the European Parliament reflects a fundamental ambiguity in the design of the European Communities (EC).[3] The founders of the EC were deeply divided over what they intended the new organization to be: some favoured something close to a supranational federation; others favoured cooperation on a more intergovernmental basis. The result was a compromise between these two extreme positions, with the European Parliament representing a symbol of the EC's democratic pretensions, but without the powers usually associated with parliaments in liberal democracies. It possessed no real legislative powers and, despite supervisory powers over the European Commission, it had scant opportunity to hold the Community's executive to account. However, this gradually changed as the EP gained both power and influence, shifting, as Otto Schmuck (1989) put it, 'from a forum for discussion to a co-player' in European politics. The rationale for such changes generally hinged on the argument that the European Parliament offered the European Union democratic legitimacy. This claim was made by Members of the European Parliament (MEPs) seeking to increase their own powers, but was accepted by the other institutions, including the Council, and by Member State governments acting through intergovernmental conferences (IGCs), who gradually conceded more powers to the Parliament as the EC/U's competences expanded. Such arguments were used before the introduction in 1979 of direct elections, but were more potent thereafter. Prior to direct election the European Parliament had only an indirect legitimacy, with members nominated by national governments. Direct elections altered the basis of legitimation by giving voters an opportunity to choose their representatives.

This book concludes that the expectations of Monnet, Hallstein and others have been only partially fulfilled: elections to the European Parliament have not conferred the legitimacy expected. This is due partly to a failure of European elites to carry their mass publics with them: some of the disaffected demonstrated their dissatisfaction by failing to vote in EP elections. However, it is still only 20 years since the first direct elections were held and so perhaps it is rather soon to expect public participation in such elections to begin to resemble that in national political communities which have taken decades or even

---

3.   The term 'European Community/ies' is used for references to the period before the entry into force in 1993 of the Treaty on European Union (TEU), which established the European Union (EU).

centuries to mature. Thus, it might be possible to see the gradual evolution of the European Parliament and the experience of direct elections as a step towards a transnational democracy, but one that, as of 1999, did not more than superficially resemble democracy as practised in most Western states.

Background

Questions of democracy beyond the national level do not just arise from the process of formal integration. They are partly a result of increasing economic interdependence that has affected states in the late twentieth century. Such changes have effectively diminished the differences between domestic and foreign policy, frequently giving rise to a situation in which national politicians cannot legislate effectively in many issue areas, such as pollution, since there is no efficient way of policing such laws (Wallace 1994: xix).[4] Thus, by the late 1990s, questions of democracy and accountability 'beyond the nation state' were increasingly relevant in many parts of the world; only the Europeans had actively sought some way of overcoming such problems.

The process of European integration raises new questions of how to ensure democratic decision-making given the creation of a set of supranational institutions. Initially the integration process was elite-led, resting on the tacit support of the citizens (Lindberg and Scheingold 1970: 19, 22). Over the years, however, there has been a growing fear that European decision-making is not democratic enough. The problem, commonly known as the 'democratic deficit', was defined by the European Parliament in 1988 as

> the combination of two phenomena: (a) the transfer of powers from the Member States to the European Community; and (b) the exercise of these powers at the Community level by institutions other than the European Parliament, even though, before the transfer, the national parliaments held power to pass laws in the areas concerned.[5]

4. There is a burgeoning literature on globalization and democratization. See, *inter alia*, Held (1995) and Archibugi, Held and Köhler (1998).
5. European Parliament Report drawn up on behalf of the Committee on Institutional Affairs on the democratic deficit in the European Community (Toussaint Report): PE 111.236/fin.1, February 1988, pp. 10-11 quoted in Bogdanor (1989a: 203-204). The problem of the democratic deficit was discussed as early as 1963 in the Janssens Report on the evolution of the Community institutions. However, it was exacerbated in the mid-1980s by the increased use of qualified majority voting

Although national parliaments can hold their own national governments to account for actions they take within the Council of Ministers (a job that is difficult and time consuming), they cannot hold the whole Council to account. MEPs therefore pressed for increased powers, arguing that only they could hold ministers responsible for decisions taken at the European level and should therefore be granted powers to ensure democratic decision-making.

There is a certain logic to this argument, which has been accepted by some national politicians: as policy areas that were traditionally the preserve of domestic politics become ever more mingled into European politics, it is increasingly difficult to ensure effective scrutiny of EU legislation. Over the years treaty changes have therefore increased the legislative powers of the European Parliament. When the Treaty on European Union (TEU) finally came into force on 1 November 1993, it conferred considerable new powers on the European Parliament. Building on the changes introduced by the Single European Act (SEA) 1986, in particular the cooperation procedure (Article 189c of the TEU), Article 189b of the TEU gave the EP the right of co-decision with the Council of Ministers in a limited number of policy areas. Coupled with an extension of the existing cooperation procedure, this represented a significant advance for the Parliament. The Treaty of Amsterdam (Article 251 TEC) went further by simplifying and extending the co-decision procedure to most areas of Community decision-making.[6]

Yet, just as Europe's elite was attempting to overcome the problems of the democratic deficit, its citizens began to express dissatisfaction with the integration process. The prime example was the Danish 'No' vote in the referendum on the Maastricht Treaty in 1992. Although the Treaty was subsequently ratified, the legitimacy of the European enterprise seemed in doubt. But what do we mean by 'democracy' and 'legitimacy'? Several interrelated concepts concerning governance have contested definitions and interpretations. This section outlines those terms that occur most often; others will be defined as they arise.

in the Council of Ministers and is compounded by a lack of transparency in EU decision-making. See Chapter 4 for further details.

6.   Here the distinction between the Community and Union is important: the powers of co-decision relate only to the first (Community) pillar of the Union, not to the more intergovernmental second or third pillars, which deal respectively with Common Foreign and Security Policy (CFSP) and Justice and Home Affairs (JHA).

Democracy

At its most basic, democracy means 'government by the people'. Yet this definition raises two further questions: what do we mean by 'government'? and what do we mean by 'the people'? (Birch 1993: 48). If government means actual participation in day-to-day decision-making, it is clear that the vast majority of citizens in the late twentieth century do not govern. However, the modern idea of representative democracy is rather less demanding, requiring citizens not to make decisions but to participate, usually by voting in periodic elections. As Jan W. van Deth (1991: 201) notes, 'some level of citizen involvement is a necessary condition for the distinction between democratic and non-democratic government'.

Yet participation is not a sufficient condition of democracy: citizens must be given an element of choice in the elections, otherwise the elections serve no more than a symbolic function of regime support. The experience of single party elections in the former Soviet-bloc countries offers a cautionary lesson in this regard: voters did turn out to vote, but the subsequent overthrow of Communist regimes across East and Central Europe casts some doubt on the significance of elections that had previously been assumed to confer legitimacy. Thus, necessary criteria for a democracy are 'free elections, a competitive party system, and a representational government' (Sartori 1968: 117-18). Such descriptions give little insight into the nature of democracy in the late twentieth century, however. Thus, for the purposes of this book, I will follow the argument of John Dunn (1992: 264) that:

> The demand to be recognised as citizens over the last three centuries and more is not best understood any longer as a demand to rule (a demand now necessarily forlorn). Rather, it should be understood as *a demand for the opportunity to make power in our adult lives always ultimately answerable to those over whom it is exercised*: a demand for the practical political means to replace subjugation by authority... (emphasis added).

Legitimacy

Max Weber argues that there are three possible sources of regime legitimacy (see Birch 1993: 33-34):[7]

7. Beetham and Lord (1998) offer a thorough analysis of the nature of legitimacy and democracy within the European Union. See also Lord (1998).

- *traditional*, based on loyalty to tribal chiefs or ruling families;
- *charismatic*, where leaders receive support for their actions because of their personal qualities. Democratically elected leaders, however charismatic, are excluded from such a category because of the legal basis of their authority;
- *legal-rational*—here regime loyalty is given to 'an impersonal set of institutions'.

Most nation states in the late twentieth century enjoy legal-rational legitimacy, which is the form the European Union would hope to attain. Such legitimacy would be most obviously demonstrated by active citizen participation in elections since, as Held (1991b: 226) asserts, 'The principle of consent, expressed through the principle of majority rule, has been...the underlying principle of legitimacy of Western democracies.' Thus, citizens are given the right to participate in elections and, by voting, they confer legitimacy on the regime.

Representation
Athenian city-state democracy in which each citizen could take part in the decision-making process has evolved into present-day representative democracy in which decisions are taken by representatives of the people. In national democracies definitions of what constituted 'the people' have gradually evolved and would now generally include adult citizens of both sexes, plus in some cases certain other adult residents. In the European Union those represented are the citizens as defined by Article 8, paragraph 1 of the TEU (Article 17, TEC), which states that 'Every person holding the nationality of a Member State shall be a citizen of the Union.' Other residents of EU Member States may also be represented according to Article 189 TEC, which states that the EP shall consist 'of representatives of the *peoples* of the States' (my emphasis).

A further question is 'what is to be represented?' Should MEPs represent states or peoples? Those who favour a Europe based on nation states assert that, to the extent that there should be a European Parliament at all, it is the states that should be represented.[8] Those with a federal vision of Europe argue that 'the peoples' must be represented.

---

8.   Several French leaders, notably President de Gaulle in the 1960s, have been reluctant to acknowledge the concept of representative democracy at the European level, preferring direct forms of democracy, especially referendums.

1. *Introduction*   17

The actual composition of the European Parliament reflects a compromise between these two positions, with seat allocation to Member States partly dependent on the relative size of the countries' populations and partly on geographic and economic size.[9]

Finally, the nature of representation is contested. There are several different ways in which people can act as representatives. The two most prevalent have been summarized as:

- *the principal-agent*—here the representative or agent (the MP) acts as the principal (or voter) wants him to do, the typical example being US Congressmen who stress their constituents' demands;
- *the representative as a trustee*—here the representative acts 'in the best interests of his constituents'. This Burkean view of representation expects representatives to act with reference to some overall concept of the nation, not specific constituencies or interests, and to act on their own judgment rather than be bound by a specific mandate or interests (Birch 1971: 37, 48).

Political Authority

Political authority 'is best defined as a combination of political power and legitimacy, where power is the ability to get things done and legitimacy is the quality of ascribed entitlement to exercise that power' (Birch 1993: 32).

Aims and Expectations of Direct Elections

Federalists who called for a directly elected European Parliament in the 1940s and early 1950s were explicitly advocating the creation of institutions of representative democracy above the national level. As Chapters 2 and 3 will show, many federalists assumed that the citizens were at least as committed as they themselves were to the concept of a federal Europe. European elections were thus seen as a way of mobilizing popular support in order to lobby national governments. By the mid-1950s it was evident that public support was not so apparent. The rationale of demands for European elections therefore shifted to claims

---

9.   For example, in 1994 Luxembourg with a population of about 400,000 had six MEPs, while Germany, with a population of 81.1 million, had 99 MEPs. For further details see Smith (1995b: 201).

that elections would elicit popular support for the process of European integration.

At no time did those who favoured direct elections question that public support could be rallied or that elections were the way to rally it. They believed that by encouraging public participation they could ensure the democratic foundations of European integration. Even those opposed to the idea of a federal Europe assumed that the introduction of elections would confer an element of democratic legitimacy which they believed belonged more properly at the national level. Fitzmaurice argues that de Gaulle's opposition to direct elections arose from a belief that they 'could only lead to an automatic increase in the powers of the Parliament and therefore an erosion of French national sovereignty' (1978: 58).

As the words of former Commission President, Walter Hallstein, suggest, there was also an implicit assumption that European elections would approximate to domestic elections on a much larger scale:

> What is lacking under the present system is an election campaign about European issues. Such a campaign would force those entitled to vote to look at and examine the questions and the various options on which the European Parliament would have to decide in the months and years ahead. It would give the candidates who emerged victorious from such a campaign a truly European mandate from their electors; and it would encourage the emergence of truly European political parties (Hallstein 1972: 74).

His argument was predicated on the idea that direct elections would be part of an embryonic European polity, with some of the trappings of democracy that exist in the nation states.

Theorists of integration also considered the nature of democracy, although most paid little attention to the citizens. Writers have typically differed over what they understand by the term 'integration', over the means of achieving integration and what the end-state would look like. In particular, differences emerge concerning whether integration is a 'condition' or a 'process' (Lindberg 1963: 4). The early theorists can be roughly divided into four categories: federalist, pluralist, functionalist and neofunctionalist (Hewstone 1986: 10). A brief glance at some of the early theories helps explain attitudes towards a directly elected parliament and the role it was expected to play.

Federalists such as the Italian former Communist Altiero Spinelli, Frenchman Denis de Rougemont and Dutchman Henrik Brugmans (who founded the College of Europe in Bruges) espoused a vision of a federal Europe: for them the end-state was clear and the means to that end-state were political. As Haas and Whiting put it:

> Federation…is the one form of unified conduct which results in the creation of a larger entity which has all the characteristics of a new national community and which is in effect a new state (1956: 452).

Yet, although this idealistic approach favoured the introduction of democratic political institutions appropriate for modern nation states, its advocates did not stress how the citizens were to become involved in the integration process. Nevertheless, federalists hoped to overcome the problems of a bureaucratic Europe by means of a directly elected Parliament to which the Commission would be responsible (Pentland 1973: 182-3).

The creation of the European Coal and Steel Community was the first step towards European integration based on 'functionalist' methods. As Karl Deutsch put it:

> The theory of *functionalism*…is based on the hope that by delegating more and more common tasks to such specific functional organizations, the world's nations will gradually become integrated into a single community within which war was impossible (1968: 166).

This approach of the ECSC has been referred to as federalism by 'small steps', but for many functionalists the point of integration was not to create a new state. Indeed, David Mitrany, the founder of functionalism, rejected:

> the federal-functionalism of Jean Monnet, whose ideas underpinned the setting up of the European Communities, on the grounds that it would simply reproduce the problems of the existence of separate states at a higher level, and thereby exacerbate rather than alleviate those problems (cited in George 1989: 8).

Rather, functionalists hoped to avert war by focusing on technical issues which they claimed were non-political.

> Integration occurs as international organizations—entirely dependent at first on national support—gradually establish their competence to perform functional tasks on their own with reference to a global social system (Pentland 1973: 76).

Functionalists accepted the existence of nation states which they did not expect to supersede; rather they sought to create their global system by establishing a technocratic network better able to fulfil the needs of citizens. People were expected to shift their loyalties as they saw the functions being tackled better at a supranational level. However, loyalties would only shift in respect of those functions being administered by the technocratic agencies, so there was no apparent threat to the nation state.

One might argue that the *ends* of European integration were federal while the *means* were Saint-Simonian, technocratic ones (Tiilikainen 1995: 25). The institutions created under Jean Monnet's guidance reflect few attempts at transposing political institutions to a European level. The European construction is technocratic in nature, ensuring for example that the Commission at least has only 'a weak and fragile democratic legitimacy' (Featherstone 1994: 150).

Neofunctionalist theories of integration—which were at their zenith in the 1950s and 1960s when academics, most of them American, sought both to explain European integration and to advise practitioners, using the EC as their case study—arose from an attempt to reconcile the federalist and functionalist approaches to European integration. Neofunctionalists viewed integration as a process. Like functionalists, they were concerned with socioeconomic functional needs; unlike functionalists, the end-state, although rarely referred to, was assumed to be a supranational state of some kind.[10] The assumption was that as problems were effectively solved above the national level, so elites would shift their loyalties to the supranational level:

> Political integration is the process whereby political actors in several distinct national settings are persuaded to shift their loyalties, expectations and political activities toward a new centre, whose institutions possess or demand jurisdiction over the pre-existing national states (Haas 1958: 16).

The actors referred to were not individual citizens, however, but rather groups of elites, who would be well placed to see the advantages of shifting their loyalties. This approach was qualitatively different from that of the federalists, since less emphasis was placed on the idea of a *democratic* European Community, than on an *efficient* Community. For

---

10. As Pentland noted in 1973, the theories altered considerably over the years with an apparent distancing from the idea of a federal end-state in the 1960s. Such shifts reflected the fact that neofunctionalists were constantly trying to describe, explain and predict the activities of the European Communities in their formative years. Neofunctionalist theories regained a considerable amount of credibility in the 1980s following the negotiation of the SEA. See Tranholm-Mikkelsen (1991).

these theorists integration could be seen to rest on a 'permissive consensus' with citizens content to follow where their elites led (Lindberg and Scheingold 1970: 41).

The idea of a federal state above the national level was anathema to pluralists. The pluralist approach asserted the supremacy of nation states as the only legitimate political actors; any activity above the national level must be conducted by sovereign nation states on an intergovernmental basis. Integration could lead to the creation of a 'community of states', supported by common attitudes, but not to a new state comprising its own institutions (Pentland 1973: 29). For pluralist theorists, including Karl Deutsch, integration could be defined as 'the growth of mutual identification among peoples' (Lindberg and Scheingold 1970: 39).

The pluralists were the only group who gave much consideration to the attitudes of citizens in the early years of integration, arguing that integration could only occur to the extent that a popular consensus emerged (Hewstone 1986:10). One leading neofunctionalist, Leon Lindberg, argued that the political actors are 'high policy-makers, civil servants, parliamentarians, interest group leaders, and other elites' (Lindberg 1963: 6-7). Neofunctionalists 'assume that identity and loyalties will gradually follow interests and expectations in clustering around and supporting institutions associated with policy integration', whereas federalists assumed that 'the creation of strong central institutions' would help foster regional identity (Nye 1968: 871). Functionalists did consider mass public opinion, but predicted that loyalties would shift in a very rational way: people would shift the focus of their loyalties when they perceived the locus of power to have altered (Pentland 1973: 84).

First- and Second-order Elections

The first direct elections failed to meet the expectations of those who had fought for their introduction: turnout in all Member States was lower than in national elections; small, new and protest parties all performed well; and the campaigns were dominated by national politicians. This scenario led Karlheinz Reif (1984a, 1984b, 1985) to describe the European Parliament elections as 'second-order', more like local elections than national general elections. Reif and Schmitt (1980) suggested that not only were EP elections second-order, they also reflected nine different national situations, and so were not unitary.

A first analysis of European election results satisfactorily justifies the assumption that European Parliament direct elections should be treated as nine simultaneous national second-order elections (Reif and Schmitt 1980: 3).

Reif's analysis is somewhat flawed by his double use of the concept of second-order elections as a way both of describing and of explaining the nature of European Parliament elections. Nevertheless, the concept of second-order elections does provide a useful framework for describing subsequent European elections, not least because it is in marked contrast to the proclaimed expectations of supporters and opponents prior to the introduction of direct elections. As Herman and Lodge (1978: 4) point out, one of the reasons that members of the Council of Ministers were reluctant to introduce direct elections was the fear that they would lead to MEPs pushing for more powers, thus reducing the role of the Council of Ministers. Ministers believed that it would be hard to deny legislative powers to a directly elected parliament, which would have legitimacy as a result of its election. The reality is that low turnout served, if anything, to increase doubts about the legitimacy of the EP (Lodge 1984: 333).

First-order elections (FOEs) are national elections in which political power is distributed at the national level (Reif 1985: 7). Depending on the political system in question they may be parliamentary (for example, the United Kingdom or the Federal Republic of Germany) or presidential (for example, the United States).[11] In general they can be seen to contribute to government formation and/or public policy formation at the *national* level.

Second-order elections (SOEs) are usually seen as less important than first-order elections, since they do not contribute directly to any change in national government or policy-making: thus it is claimed that there is 'less at stake' in such elections (Reif and Schmitt 1980: 8-9). Nevertheless, they frequently have an indirect impact. Electoral losses in *Land* elections played a part in the downfall of the ruling Social

---

11.   The situation in France is more complex since both presidential and national assembly elections may be first-order. Reif considers national assembly elections to be first-order if and only if they do *not* occur immediately after presidential elections. In line with this, my analysis will take the 1981, 1988 and 1995 presidential elections and the 1986, 1993 and 1997 parliamentary elections to be first-order. The 1981 and 1988 parliamentary elections are *not* first-order, since they came in the wake of presidential elections.

Democrat/Free Democrat Alliance in Germany in 1982 (Reif 1985: 12-13). Similarly, Michel Rocard and Achille Occhetto, the leaders of the French Socialists and Italian Party of the Democratic Left (PDS), respectively, both resigned in the wake of poor showings in the 1994 European elections. Second-order elections are distinguishable by the fact that turnout is lower than in first-order elections, and the ruling party or parties at the national level typically fare worse, while small and new parties tend to perform well (Reif 1985: 9). One difficulty in the context of European elections is that the hypothesis assumes some distinction between parties of government and opposition (Reif 1985: 12-13). This allows for coalition government, but makes an analysis of the European elections rather complex given the peculiarities of the EU as a political system. Political responsibility is so diffuse at the European level, that even when voters are aware that decisions made by the EU affect them directly, they cannot easily see who made the decisions or what policies or strategies different political groupings represent.

While the formulations used in his various publications on European and second-order elections differ slightly, Reif argues that

> The basic hypothesis of this theory is that there is a systematic relationship between the result of all sorts of SOE and the results of the FOE in a political system and this systematic relationship is based on the role political parties play in the first-order political arena (FOPA) of that system (1984b: 245).

One significant result of the predominant interest in national affairs in the minds of electors is that electoral campaigns tend not to focus solely on questions specific to the electoral arena; and this problem is compounded by the lack of an integrated European party system. Thus, for the European elections, Reif (1984b: 248) predicts that campaigns will focus on 'a mix of specific arena, i.e. EC, and of general, mostly first-order (i.e. national, domestic) arena issues'. This is in marked contrast to the expectations of Hallstein and others, who believed that such elections would lead to campaigns fought over European issues.

The European arena poses new problems: whereas other second-order elections are held at the national or subnational level, elections to the European Parliament are supranational. Thus, the elections link many national political systems—15 in 1999. Political parties seeking to cooperate must therefore form federations or be created afresh specifically for the European arena. This theme fits in well with

Hallstein's views of the European elections, since he assumed that such elections would lead to the formation of transnational political parties (Hallstein 1972: 74). In this context, a further interesting point needs to be considered:

> Although clearly of second-order nature, the European Community links several national (first-order) political systems with each other. The legitimacy of political parties playing an active and important role in what traditionally has been the arena of diplomats thinking in terms of national, and not of partisan, interests, might be less (Reif and Schmitt 1980: 11).

All things being equal, this may lead to reluctance on the part of voters to participate in European elections.

In the European context the problem is further complicated by the concept of government at the European level remaining blurred. While there is 'less at stake' in second-order elections within states there is, as already pointed out, *something* at stake; Reif and Schmitt (1980: 12) are less certain that anything is at stake in European elections, since they only serve to select the personnel for a weak parliamentary institution, with decision-making power lying elsewhere. The situation had clearly changed by 1999: the European Parliament enjoyed considerable legislative powers and in January of that year it came close to sacking the European Commission. If the introduction of a right of co-decision agreed at Maastricht in 1991 and its extension in the Treaty of Amsterdam of 1997 did not make much impact on the public's perception of the EP, the vote of censure on the Commission in January 1999 and its resignation two months later was a different matter, bringing the Parliament to the forefront of media attention and demonstrating its powers. The Commission's resignation did not immediately follow the Parliament's vote, but came very soon after publication of the Report of the Committee of Independent Experts, demanded by the Parliament (EP 1999d) and which found evidence of maladministration and cronyism in the Commission. Had the Commission not resigned, MEPs would undoubtedly have held another vote of censure, which would almost certainly have gone against the Commission. Thus, the Parliament played an important part in the demise of the Commission, even if it did not sack it directly. However, even though the powers of the EP had increased, the complex and opaque procedure inevitably made it difficult to explain the role played by the EP.

Outline

Demands for a European Parliamentary Assembly can be traced back to the 1948 Congress of Europe at The Hague. The outcome was the Parliamentary Assembly of the Council of Europe, a much weaker body than the federalists had envisaged. Yet the creation of even a limited parliamentary body was significant in setting a precedent when the European Communities were established. Moreover, the debates at The Hague prefigured many of those characterizing the integration process in Europe.

Chapter 2 outlines the debates surrounding the creation of a European Parliament, arguing that the reasoning behind such demands was largely federalist in nature: the goal of European integration was political and an assembly was symbolic of aspirations for a project designed to unite the 'peoples'. Conversely, the so-called 'Gaullist approach', favoured by the British and Scandinavians as well as some French, was to create a Europe of nation states. This concept of Europe saw no place for a supranational assembly, since it believed that the nation state was the only legitimate locus of political power.

Chapter 3 focuses on calls for direct elections for the European Parliament. It analyses the arguments for enlarging the powers of Parliament and the apparent 'gordian knot' of whether to enlarge those powers before the introduction of direct elections or whether only a directly elected body could be the recipient of increased powers.

Chapter 4 considers the European Parliament's powers and influence in terms of their significance for EU decision-making. The assumption that it is less important than national parliaments is partially challenged by an analysis of the powers at the EP's disposal. However, further evidence suggests that, while the EP does have several legislative and other functions that render it in some respects as powerful as some of its national counterparts, it lacks the support typically enjoyed by the parliaments in the Member States although increasing use of its powers might serve to increase its support.

Right from the start, members of the Common Assembly sat in transnational party groups alongside members from sister parties from other states, rather than in national delegations. This decision symbolized MEPs' determination that the integration process should go beyond intergovernmental cooperation. When the European Council finally took the decision in 1974 to hold direct elections, the main party families—the Christian Democrats, Socialists and Liberals—formalized their relations by creating transnational party federations, which officially became parties in the 1990s. Chapter 5 outlines the relationship between national and European-level political parties and party groups within the European Parliament. It is argued that transnational parties have emerged, but that they cannot be seen as analogous to national political parties—the two serve complementary functions.

Chapter 6 demonstrates that the reality of European elections has not matched the expectations of the federalists or the fears of the Gaullists. The first four sets of European elections saw low and falling levels of participation, leading many commentators to question support for the integration process more generally. Moreover, results reflected the national electoral climates in the various Member States, with voters typically voting for or against national political parties (or, more realistically, for or against national governments). Only in Denmark has the situation differed markedly from the pattern described. Since the first referendum on joining the then European Community in 1972, Danish political parties have campaigned in European elections and referendums on the basis of support or opposition to further European integration. Thus, in Denmark, many of the standard criticisms of EP elections, such as the lack of choice over issues relating to the nature of integration, do not hold. The 1994 elections saw an increase in the amount of choice offered to voters elsewhere in the Union, with the emergence of the *L'Autre Europe* list in France and the rather less successful Referendum Party in Britain. Yet such choices as were available were negative in spirit—voters could vote for or against further integration, but there was little or no scope for voting on the *way* the integration process should proceed. Chapter 6 gives a statistical analysis of the results and turnout of the first four sets of direct elections, showing how far the elections met the expectations of the founding fathers and the fears of the intergovernmentalists, and where they failed to do so.

European elections have fallen far short of the expectations (and fears) of politicians and commentators prior to the first elections in 1979. Yet, despite the apparent failure of expectations, by 1999 Europe's elected Parliament had begun to play a vital part in European decision-making. The practice of democracy 'beyond the nation state' differed from that in national states, but the elections had become an important part of the European Union's political processes.

2 |

The Origins of the European Parliament: 1948–58

Demands for the creation of a European Parliament must be seen in the context of the postwar peace settlement. As politicians and other elites sought ways of rendering war impossible, the idea of a parliamentary body was advocated as a method of conferring democratic legitimacy on the various schemes for establishing peace. There was no single set of ideas underpinning the creation of the European Communities, still less of the Parliament. Two main strands of thought can be seen running through the negotiations: the Monnet-style technocratic approach, which saw little need for a parliamentary assembly; and the federalist approach favoured by Altiero Spinelli and Henrik Brugmans, for whom an assembly was an important part of the symbolism of the federation they hoped to create. From 1958 onwards, these two approaches, which were both in favour of a closely integrated Europe, faced opposition from de Gaulle who insisted on a Europe of nation states. As the next chapter demonstrates, many expectations about the evolution of the Parliament were shared by federalists and Gaullists alike, the chief difference lying in whether such expectations were viewed positively or negatively.

Following The Hague Congress of 1948, which gave the impetus to the founding of the Council of Europe, there were repeated calls for a representative European assembly. The establishment of the Council of Europe Consultative Assembly in 1949 in some ways paved the way for the creation of the European Parliament: the debates at The Hague Congress, the issues raised there, and the outcome all prefigured many of the arguments concerning the European Parliament.

The Idea of a United Europe

The process of formal European integration can only be understood in the context of the postwar socioeconomic situation in Europe. Few

European countries had been spared invasion and all West European states were aware of a need to rebuild their economies and their states.[1] Three factors in particular added weight to calls for a European federation or a united Europe.[2] First, there was a growing awareness that changes in the world economy were rendering national economies unviable. The Preamble to the Preliminary Report of the Congress of The Hague saw the shift towards an integrated Europe as the logical, but unrealized, result of the 'age of oil', just as the age of steam had led to the consolidation of the nation state in the nineteenth century. Secondly, there was a great sense of fear surrounding threats to security from a resurgent Germany and from an expansionist Communist Soviet Union. These issues combined to give a sense of urgency to the European project and led many to assert that the nation state was no longer adequate for solving the problems of the twentieth century:

> In the economic field, the conditions which gave rise to the contemporary Nation-States of Europe no longer exist... Not one single European country to-day is, by itself, an effective political or economic unit...
>   The creation of a United Europe offers the only possible solution to the economic and political problems which confront us (Preamble to Congress of Europe at The Hague, 1948e).

Thirdly, the United States provided both overt and covert support for a federal Europe (Aldrich 1995). For the Americans the dangers of European Communism and the need to reintegrate Germany into a stable Western Europe contributed to a willingness to provide financial aid in the form of the Marshall Plan. Many Congressmen hoped that the Organization for European Economic Cooperation (OEEC), established in 1948, would become an 'embryo of a federal state', a model they pushed hard in their subsequent dealings with the Europeans. As Harper (1996: 66) argues, 'It was only natural for them [the Americans]

---

1.   The fact that Britain had not been invaded contributed to the reluctance of its leaders to take part in formal initiatives of European integration.
2.   Both terms were used with great regularity. Winston Churchill made frequent calls for Europe to unite, in particular in his 'United States of Europe' speech in Zürich in 1946. Many participants at the Congress of the Hague, notably Henrik Brugmans and Denis de Rougemont, favoured a federation. 'Federation', 'uniting' and the even vaguer 'European integration' were all deliberately ambiguous terms. Churchill was never explicit as to what he understood by the concept of a united Europe, whereas Brugmans was quite clear that it entailed a European government and parliament (Congress of Europe at The Hague 1948d).

to insist—once they had decided to make an unprecedented financial commitment—that the "something" resemble the United States'.

The idea of a united Europe was not just a result of the Second World War (Smith and Stirk 1990). Many attempts to unite Europe by force have been made over the centuries, including those by Charlemagne and Bismarck. The expansionist German National Socialists of the 1930s were the most pertinent to postwar sentiment. Yet, there are also many early examples of idealists who believed that by establishing a federal Europe, one could avoid war. Urwin (1991: 2) notes that the English Quaker, William Penn, was calling for a European parliament in 1693. Already during the Second World War several resistance movements had begun to call for a European federation aimed at preserving peace in Europe (Corbett 1998: 3-5). However, the post-war period saw the first substantive moves towards voluntary, institutionalized cooperation among sovereign nation states going beyond mere international agreements.

Owing to a proliferation of federalist movements in the years immediately following the Second World War, an attempt was made to rationalize the groups by the formation in December 1947 of the International Committee of the Movements for European Unity.[3] Thus representatives of the major groups campaigning for European integration—*Conseil Français pour l'Europe Unie, Ligue Indépendante de Coopération Européenne, Nouvelles Equipes Internationales, Union Européenne des Fédéralistes, Union Parlementaire Européenne* and *United Europe Movement*—jointly organized the Conference in The Hague in May 1948 under the auspices of the Committee.

The Congress of Europe at The Hague, 1948

The conference brought together 750 people, including former ministers and prime ministers from European states, and observers from the United States and the British Commonwealth. In his speech to the closing plenary, Duncan Sandys, a British Conservative and son-in-law of Winston Churchill, referred to the Congress as 'the most representative assembly of independent citizens that has ever met to deliberate

---

3. The European Movement became a major recipient of covert financial aid from the United States Central Intelligence Agency (CIA) via the American Committee on United Europe, created in 1948 just for this purpose (Aldrich 1995: 161-62).

upon the fate of Europe'.[4] Admittedly, self-selection meant that the representative nature of the conference was doubtful; nevertheless there were some very clear expositions of the issues surrounding European cooperation and possible institutional arrangements for a federal Europe.

Speakers stressed the urgency of their actions, without which they felt Europe would be doomed. As Denis de Rougemont (1948) put it, 'We are here to declare the urgency of a voluntary union of the peoples of Europe arising from a great peril and a greater hope' (my translation). The first reason for action—growing economic interdependence—was felt to render the nation state inadequate for the needs of postwar reconstruction, necessitating international cooperation of some sort. Several speakers expressed the feeling that the need for economic integration made political integration inevitable. Secondly, perceived threats to security from both Russia and Germany led to calls for federation, since it was felt that only united could Europe avoid being 'submerged under the advancing tide of totalitarian dictatorship'. Here again American influence was evident: US politicians were especially concerned about the dangers of Communism and at that time the Communists were the largest single parties in both France and Italy (Camps 1964: 5; Hogan 1987). These themes led to ideas concerning a political union since, as Sandys (1947: paragraph 1) had noted earlier, 'no far-reaching measures of economic integration are possible without some corresponding unification in the political and military spheres'.

American influence was discernible both in the models for a federal polity, based on the United States, and also because of American demands for close European cooperation. In one speech to the Congress, the veteran European federalist, Count Richard Coudenhove-Kalergi (1948) even quoted a letter from US Senator J. W. Fulbright:

> The one way that the people of Europe can repay the American people for their sacrifices in two wars and in the American Recovery Programme, is to overcome their ancient nationalism, recognize their

4.   As Miriam Camps (1964: 6 n. 7) notes, the British and Scandinavians typically had a 'functionalist' view of European integration, hoping to achieve 'European "unity" by intergovernmental co-operation on specific points, while the French, Italian and Benelux delegates were usually "federalists"'. One active exception representing Britain was R.W.G. (Kim) Mackay. A Labour MP from New Zealand, he was a committed federalist whose work was supported by the American Committee on United Europe (Aldrich 1995: 168).

identity of interests and create a living, vital European Community, able once more, as they have in the past, to contribute to the forward march of Western Christian civilization.

What is particularly striking is both the zeal with which those attending the Congress approached the question of uniting Europe and the belief that this was the will of the people of Europe. In the words of the Belgian politician Paul Van Zeeland:

> This Congress has a mission: it is to answer the prayer of the masses of Europe; to give more precise and more concrete expression to their aspirations; to show the governments that even if they are daring in conception, public opinion will follow them, if indeed it is not already ahead of them (European Movement 1949: 22).

This then was not the elitist approach of which Monnet would later be accused: federalists genuinely felt that the people were behind them and where this was in any doubt they saw the necessity of winning popular support. Nor was the project of a united Europe viewed merely as a way to assuage short-term problems; rather the drafters of the Political Report to the Congress argued that 'it meets the requirements of permanent conditions of modern life'.

But what sort of Europe did those present at the Congress envisage, what institutions did they deem vital and what methods did they feel to be appropriate? The Congress was divided into three Committees, one each dealing with political, economic and social, and cultural affairs. Only the proposals emerging from the Political Committee are considered in detail here.

The Proposals of the Congress
The Political Committee called for a 'voluntary federation' of democratic states which none would be forced to join.[5] Moreover, while it envisaged the transfer of sovereignty to a central organization it also favoured limits to activity at the federal level, constrained by the extent of 'common interest'. The Committee called for a European Assembly to be convened as soon as possible, since members were convinced that 'the stir created by its convening will create considerable strength by awakening hope and will lead the organization to further progress'. The

5.   Material in this paragraph is taken from the International European Movement Papers held in the European Communities Archives at the European University Institute in Florence.

preliminary proposals had called for a European Deliberative Assembly 'through which views could be exchanged and a common European opinion expressed on the major problems of the day', but saw the creation of 'an elected European Parliament with legislative powers' as a possibility for the future. The final Resolution called for a European Assembly:

> 8) ...the convening, as a matter of real urgency, of a European Assembly chosen by the Parliaments of the participating nations, from among their members and others, designed
>
>   a) to stimulate and give expression to European public opinion;
>
>   b) to advise upon immediate practical measures designed progressively to bring about the necessary economic and political union of Europe;
>
>   c) to examine the juridical and constitutional implications arising out of the creation of such a Union or Federation and their economic and social consequences;
>
>   d) to prepare the necessary plans for the above purposes.

The role of the assembly would be to mobilize public support; further powers were not laid out in the report. Thus it was not envisaged that the European Assembly would form the legislative arm of a European federation, nor yet that it should be a Constituent Assembly whose task would be to 'frame the European institutions', since either would be premature. Rather, its task was to be that of 'studying and drawing up plans of a general nature for co-operation and more particularly the fundamental statutes'.

The original proposal favoured the selection of members of the assembly from among the members of national parliaments, but this idea did not win universal support. As one representative pointed out, 'MPs have a mandate for domestic policy, not to make European policy' (my translation). A range of amendments was therefore proposed. Paul Reynaud, a former French prime minister, called for direct elections within six months, on the basis of one member per million voters, arguing that a European Assembly composed of national MPs would have no European mandate and do little to stimulate public support (European Movement 1949: 27). Similarly, the French parliamentarian and later minister, Edouard Bonnefous, felt that in the absence of direct elections there would be no mandate for the merging of sovereignties that the Committee deemed necessary (European Movement 1949: 27).

Those who favoured Europe-wide direct elections did so as a way of harnessing the public support which they felt already existed for a

European federation (Count Coudenhove-Kalergi noted that a Gallup Poll indicated strong public support for a European federation) and as a way of articulating the demands of the citizens of Europe, since ideally people would vote not as Frenchmen or Germans, but as Europeans. The Belgian Paul-Henri Spaak in particular exhorted the elites to press ahead, arguing that the citizens were already supporting European integration (European Movement 1949: 27). Reynaud's idea of direct elections offered scope for the representation of people rather than states, with equal representation for all citizens as individuals, regardless of their nationality. This notion led to anxiety among some representatives from the smaller states who disliked the idea of their state being outvoted. Dr Brugmans from The Netherlands argued that the idea of one member for every million inhabitants ran the risk of creating a 'superstate' which would ignore the basic regional, national and functional communities and ought to be rejected. Some delegates therefore favoured a two chamber system, with one chamber to represent the states, the other the people.

Others argued for an amendment that would lead members to be chosen not by national MPs only but also by representatives of various social, professional and cultural groups in each Member State, in order that the assembly be more representative of the countries.[6] In the event both amendments were rejected, but a compromise was reached whereby the nominees were to be chosen by national parliaments but did not themselves have to be members of parliament.

The decision did not rule out direct elections in the future for a European Parliament, but, as the final report noted, it reflected several thoughts: that direct elections might take a long time to introduce and that direct representation might lead to strong centralizing tendencies, since parliaments chosen by universal suffrage were the most authoritative expression of the will of the people. Moreover, as Kim Mackay pointed out, while the idea of a directly elected parliament was laudable, direct elections for this initial consultative body would make the Congress look very foolish. In the short term it was more important to work with national parliaments which alone, as the French Socialist

---

6.   This approach is indicative of the 'functionalist' representation favoured by several strands of continental thought at the time, including Catholic social doctrine and some forms of socialist thought. Similar proposals were made when the ECSC Treaty was drafted. Functional representation persists in the form of the EU's Economic and Social Committee (ECOSOC).

Paul Ramadier pointed out, had the right to cede part of their sovereignty to a supranational entity (European Movement 1949: 34).

Despite the perceived urgency of the federalists' cause, the proposals resulting from the Congress of Europe were evolutionary rather than revolutionary. While some participants favoured the immediate creation of a federal Europe with directly elected institutions, this was seen by the majority as a longer term project. However, partly as a result of the stimulus of the Congress and of American demands for closer cooperation between European states, a Council of Europe with an intergovernmental Council of Ministers and a Consultative Assembly was established in 1949 (Mackay 1951).

While the creation of the Council of Europe was hoped by many to be a step towards a European federation, they were to be disappointed.

> In the Council of Europe, those who spoke for the federalist movement dreamed of a parliamentary revolution, a 'Saint Bartholomew's Night' of national sovereignties, a sort of 'Tennis Court Oath'. The lesson has painfully to be learned that an assembly can do nothing effective unless it has a government answerable to it. And the cold fact was that the 'Consultative Assembly' at Strasbourg was hardly ever 'consulted' at all (Brugmans 1970: 11).

Nevertheless, the implications of the Congress's demands and the creation of the Council go further than this. Pierre Gerbet (1992: 12) has argued that, 'Once the Council of Europe included a parliamentary assembly, it was inconceivable that the first European Community should not have one.' How far does this assertion explain the creation of the Common Assembly of the ECSC?

The Schuman Plan and the Treaty of Paris, 1950–51

The fears and anxieties about the future of European security, economic and physical, which proved such a motivating force prior to the Congress of The Hague, did not diminish in the following two years.[7] Indeed, they were compounded by the belief that the constraints imposed by the Allies on Germany since 1945 would soon be lifted, giving rise to the possibility of instability caused by a reinvigorated Germany, which might lead to renewed international conflict. More-

---

7. This section and the next draw particularly on material found in the Pierre Uri Papers in the European Communities Archives at the European University Institute in Florence.

over, unfulfilled demanz for coal gave economic reasons for closer cooperation with Germany, which was the chief supplier of the commodity to France. Thus security and economic questions, which traditional international cooperation seemed unable to tackle effectively, again gave an impetus to proposals for European integration, this time in the form of the Schuman Plan.[8]

On 9 May 1950, the French Foreign Minister, Robert Schuman, called for the pooling of coal and steel production as the first stage of economic integration, leading ultimately to a European federation. The Plan, which led to the creation of the European Coal and Steel Community, contained several interrelated proposals, designed to make war between France and Germany 'not only unthinkable, but materially impossible'. This would be achieved by putting all French and German coal and steel production, plus that of any other country that chose to join, under a common High Authority.

The Schuman Plan envisaged this pooling of production as the first stage of a European federation that would be indispensable to the preservation of peace. The provision for the creation of a supranational High Authority was an important innovation, since the new institution was to be endowed with certain limited powers, delegated by the Member States. This went beyond traditional international organizations in which constraints on national sovereignty or at least autonomy arise as a result of necessary interaction; in the ECSC, the delegation of sovereignty was to be a deliberate act on the part of Member States, enabling the High Authority to act independently of national governments.

The idea of 'pooling sovereignty' was a factor in British reluctance to join the proposed Community, since the British were unwilling to commit themselves until they knew what would be entailed. However, other countries considered that traditional international organizations were inadequate to tackle the problems facing the nation states of Western Europe and accepted the need for some loss of sovereignty. The Luxembourg delegation to the negotiations that drafted the Treaty of Paris argued that the problem with many international organizations was that they could not execute the tasks assigned to them because they

---

8. Ironically, in the light of de Gaulle's subsequent, rather deleterious, impact on the integration process, Jean Monnet (1951: 3) argued strongly that traditional methods had failed owing to the tendency of states to assert their 'national interests'.

lacked adequate powers. This 'partial fusion of sovereignty', as the French called it, was to be the catalyst for the creation of the first international assembly which was more than simply a consultative body.

In the wake of Schuman's declaration, a committee of French experts was formed to draft a working document. The text was presented to delegates from Germany, Italy and the Benelux countries on 27 June 1950 and formed the basis of the Treaty of Paris establishing the European Coal and Steel Community. The experts proposed institutions that could be seen as 'the embryo of federal institutions for Europe', consisting as they did of a supranational High Authority, a supranational Court of Justice, a Council of Ministers to represent the states and a Common Assembly to represent the peoples. However, the institutional arrangements owed little to the sort of federalist zeal that had motivated many of those present at the Congress of The Hague.

The approach envisaged by Schuman and the French experts was one of 'functional' integration, in which successful integration in one policy area would be followed by integration in a related area. The Luxembourg delegation pointed out that although this method would be slower than a federalist approach, it had the advantage of giving effective results while at the same time permitting integration to progress. Thus the aim was to create institutions for the efficient coordination of activity in a specific policy area or, as the Luxembourgers put it, to form 'a genuinely single state in the field of coal and steel' (my translation).

The High Authority was deemed to be the crucial institution within this scheme, while the idea of a Common Assembly appears to have been at most a virtue made out of necessity. Since establishing a supranational High Authority entailed a 'fusion of sovereignties', the question arose of how to keep this new institution accountable; a Common Assembly composed of delegations from the various national parliaments was deemed to be the 'least imperfect solution' to the problem (Schuman Plan 1950a). The working group's original draft called for national parliaments to select members of the Common Assembly; no provision for direct elections was envisaged. Thus the Assembly was to represent the citizens of the Member States; at the same time national parliaments which relinquished part of their sovereignty would exercise these sovereign powers jointly. Some countries argued for direct election of Members of the Common Assembly and Article 20 of the Treaty of Paris allowed individual Member States to decide whether to have direct elections or allow national parliaments to select the Members.

Although nominally the parliamentary branch of the Community, the Common Assembly's role was more limited than that of most national parliaments. The Assembly was a mechanism for scrutiny and account-ability, not a legislative body in any sense: its only significant power was 'supervisory', aimed at controlling the High Authority (Article 24 of the Treaty of Paris). This supervisory power was to be exercised through the hearing of an annual report from the High Authority, followed by a debate and the right to oust the entire High Authority by a two-thirds and absolute majority of members. Since the activities of the High Authority were limited to the spheres of coal and steel, the Assembly's powers were similarly limited in scope.

The Assembly was not granted any legislative powers, and a proposal put forward by the French that following a two-thirds majority vote it should be allowed to ask for the withdrawal of a decision or recommendation of the High Authority, did not win the support of other delegations. The feeling of the delegations was that the Council of Ministers would work with the High Authority *before* decisions were taken, with the Common Assembly *after*.

The Assembly was not part of a blueprint for a European federation based on parliamentary principles. It has sometimes been argued that the institutions and division of powers established by the Treaty of Paris were inspired by the democratic tradition of the separation of powers, yet this does not characterize the ECSC adequately either. Rather the proposals were seen as the best way of tackling questions arising from the creation of a supranational authority, themselves occurring because of a sense that national institutions were no longer adequate to deal with Europe's problems. Thus, even if it is tempting to view the proposals as an attempt to create a supranational federation based on principles used in existing national federal systems, that was not the prime objective of the founders.

What was established was, in the words of Jean Monnet (1951), 'A new sort of relationship between states, with powers delegated to an authority which can act in the interest of all' (my translation). It is in this context that the role of the Common Assembly must be viewed. Certainly it was not granted the powers to be the legislative body of the Community; that was not the intention. François Duchêne (1994: 240), noting French hostility to the German idea of a supranational

Assembly, has described Monnet's approach to the Assembly at that time as one of a 'technocratic minimalist'. How far the situation had evolved after more than 40 years of formal European integration will be considered in the final chapter. Next, however, the idea of a 'Green Pool' which was briefly floated by the French will be outlined, since it raises ideas about the way the process of integration was expected to move.

A First Attempt to Extend Integration: The Green Pool of 1950

In line with the views held by the framers of the Treaty of Paris—that the pooling of coal and steel production should be but the first step in economic integration, leading to political integration and ultimately federation—the French Agriculture Minister, Pierre Pflimlin, floated the idea of an agricultural community or 'Green Pool'. Indeed, the proposals seemed entirely in accordance with the hopes of those who felt that the concrete results of coal and steel integration would lead to popular support for further cooperation. Thus Pflimlin proposed capitalizing on the popularity of the coal and steel project in Europe and in French opinion to take a new initiative that would help both the French agricultural sector and European economic unification.

In accordance with the ideas underpinning the Schuman Plan, Pflimlin proposed the creation of a European agricultural institution comparable with the ECSC's High Authority, which would be accountable to the Common Assembly to be established when the Schuman Plan was implemented. Similarly, the proposed Agricultural Community would have shared the ECSC's Court of Justice. This again was entirely in line with the intention that the institutional structure of the ECSC should allow for the creation of additional functional communities.

The Head of the General Planning Commission, Jean Monnet, expressed his support for the proposition, noting that the Court and Assembly would remain viable for a new Community, while the Council and High Authority would not, owing to their technical nature. For Monnet (1951: 2) the latter two institutions prefigured 'a genuine ministerial department based on federal principles' (my translation).

In the end the Green Pool came to nothing, impeded by the British, Irish, Swedish, Swiss and Norwegians, who would not accept a supranational authority in this policy sector. Yet the fact that the agricultural community was proposed at all and the nature of the institutional patterns suggested are indicative of elite attitudes towards European integration in the early 1950s and of the Common Assembly's role. The high point of enthusiasm for a European Assembly was to show itself in proposals for a European Defence Community (EDC) and an associated European Political Community (EPC). Also doomed to failure, this project was nevertheless significant in terms of the issues it raised concerning the nature of a supranational parliament, representation above the level of the nation state, and the possibility of transnational democracy.

Proposals for a European Political Community: 1952–54

In marked contrast to earlier conferences considering ways of integrating Europe, the Ad Hoc Assembly was established in 1952 at the behest of national *governments* for the specific purpose of drawing up proposals for a European Political Community. In the wake of the Schuman Plan and the creation of the European Coal and Steel Community, a proposal had been made for a European Defence Community and a treaty was signed on 30 May 1952.[9] Article 38 of the European Defence Community Treaty called for the proposed EDC Assembly (modelled on the ECSC Assembly) to

> examine the constitution of an Assembly of the European Defence Community, elected on a democratic basis, and to define the powers which would be vested in such an Assembly, and the changes which might have to be made in consequence in the EDC Treaty, while bearing in mind that this permanent organization of the Defence Community should be able to constitute one of the elements in a subsequent federal or confederal structure (Benvenuti Report 1952: 6).

This implied a delay until the EDC Treaty was ratified and its assembly constituted. Rather than wait, the Consultative Assembly of the Council of Europe voted on the day the Treaty was signed for work to start on a European Political Community before ratification of the EDC Treaty was complete. This demand was followed on 10 September 1952 by the *Luxembourg Resolution*, in which ministers meeting in a special Council of Ministers requested the Members of the Common Assembly to draw up a draft treaty instituting a European Political Community

9. For details of the background to the EDC and EPC, see Fursdon (1980) and Cardozo (1987).

(Benvenuti Report 1952: 7). Nine additional members were co-opted onto the Common Assembly in order to make the numbers up to those of the proposed EDC Assembly. This so-called 'Ad Hoc Assembly' created a Constitutional Committee of 26 members.[10] A smaller working group was subsequently set up to produce a working programme prior to the sessions of the Constitutional Committee. There was considerable disagreement even over the name of the Committee, since some felt 'Constitutional' was too strong.

The tasks set out by the EDC Treaty and the Luxembourg Resolution were deemed to fall into three categories: the scope of Community action, the institutions, and relations with international organizations. Three sub-committees were set up to deal with these areas, with the institutional sub-committee being further divided to create sub-sub-committees on judicial affairs and on political institutions.

Article 38 put forward certain fundamental principles for a European Political Community:

- an Assembly elected on a democratic basis,
- a two-Chamber representative system,
- the separation of powers,
- suitable representation of the States (Benvenuti Report 1952: para. 6c)

which set the framework for the Constitutional Committee's work. Given these conditions, a federal system of some sort was the inevitable outcome of the negotiations, although members of the Committee proved reluctant to follow the requirement in Article 38 to consider the relative merits of different forms of federal and confederal states, especially since, as Fernand Dehousse pointed out, each state develops its own federalism, which derives from its own sense of history, not from stereotypical juridical ideas (Ad Hoc Assembly 1952c: 12). Those who sought a federal solution to the question of a European political order assumed that such a federation was possible, not considering potential differences from existing federal states at the national level, nor whether the concept of a federal state composed of previously sovereign nation states would be feasible.

However, while there was a general belief that the outcome should be a federal Europe, howsoever defined, some representatives did hold markedly differing views. The most notable dissenter was Michel

10. This section draws on the Minutes and Reports of the Ad Hoc Assembly, which are located in the European Communities Archives in Florence.

Debré, a Gaullist, who prefigured the problems for European integration created by de Gaulle himself. Debré believed that a European parliament would have to be the emanation of national parliaments, with the European executive depending on the legitimacy of national parliaments. As he put it, 'A political federation can only be based on national governments and parliaments' (Ad Hoc Assembly 1952c: 32-33 [my translation]). This oppositional strand of French thinking did not persuade the Committee seriously to consider proposals for a political community based on nation states; it opted for one with supranational elements as in the two existing or proposed Communities—Coal and Steel, and Defence.

One crucial question was raised concerning the sphere of competence of the new Community: would it encompass just the spheres of the ECSC and the EDC or would it go further? A second important question was the form that the European Assembly would take. In this context both the composition of the two chambers and the methods for selecting their members were to be considered.

In addition, discussions took place concerning the precise nature of representation in each of the two chambers. The final wording put forward by the sub-committee on Political Institutions (Benvenuti *et al.* 1952: Article 8) was a compromise offering a first chamber (Chamber of the People) composed of representatives of the people and a second chamber (Senate) comprising representatives of the states. The Working Group unanimously agreed that the first chamber had to be elected by universal suffrage and argued that its members should be considered as representatives of Europe and not of their constituencies, just as members of national parliaments are representatives of the nation (Ad Hoc Assembly 1952i: paras. 15, 17). This particularly French view of representation was accepted by the Committee in its final report.

It is interesting to note that the idea of direct elections was therefore floated, in part, as the rational response to a problem related to the EDC, rather than a deliberate attempt to move towards a federal union. If the EDC Treaty was to be ratified by the French Parliament, it was essential to secure the support of the Socialists, who demanded 'a more "democratic" EDC with a European Assembly elected by universal suffrage' (Duchêne 1994: 234). Differences of opinion emerged over methods of selecting the second chamber, but there was general agreement that it should not just be a council of national ministers.

Had they been accepted, the Ad Hoc Assembly's proposals would have created the institutional underpinnings for a federal Europe based on the separation of powers. However, plans for a European Political Community collapsed when the French Parliament failed to ratify the EDC Treaty in 1954. Since the legal basis for the Political Community was grounded in Article 38 of that Treaty, albeit supported by subsequent declarations of the Council of Ministers, it was not possible to press on with formal political integration: the high point of European federalism seemed to have passed.

Messina, Spaak and the Treaties of Rome: 1955–57

After the failure to ratify the EDC Treaty, Monnet and the Belgian Foreign Minister, Paul-Henri Spaak, were quick to assert the need for a *relance européenne*.[11] An intergovernmental conference was convened at Messina in June 1955, and a Committee was created under Spaak's chairmanship. The outcome of this was the creation of an Economic Community and an Atomic Energy Community, each based broadly on the pattern introduced in the Coal and Steel Community. Monnet himself favoured extending the sectoral approach to include nuclear power, although the final result of this new move towards European integration—the creation of a 'common market' alongside an Atomic Energy Community—went considerably further than Monnet's more limited concept of 'sectoral integration'. Nevertheless, the institutional arrangements proposed were remarkably similar to those of the Coal and Steel Community.

The underlying aim of those organizing the Conference at Messina— as outlined in a preparatory document written prior to the opening of the Conference—was to create a United States of Europe based on the development of common institutions. The institutions proposed in the document—an Assembly, a Council of Ministers, a 'Common Organ' which was to be roughly analogous to the High Authority, and the Court—had their pattern in the ECSC. However, in line with one of the ideas proposed by the Ad Hoc Assembly, elections to the Assembly by direct universal suffrage were envisaged as soon as the scope of the Assembly's activities was large enough. Thus, the idea that the Community's Assembly should be subject to direct election, which had met with only limited support in 1950, seemed by 1955 to have prevailed.

11. This paragraph draws on Duchêne (1994: 262-69).

However, the Spaak Committee's proposals of 8 November 1955 took a step back. Arguing for an enlargement of the ECSC Assembly's powers to enable it to exert control over the new Economic Community, the Committee declared its support for an increase in the number of members of the Assembly, which would also help to bring more *national* MPs into contact with the development of Europe. Direct election was not mentioned, rather the proposal said that national parliaments should choose the members of the European Assembly (Spaak Committee 1955). The final outcome did propose that provision should be made for the direct election of the Parliamentary Assembly via Article 138(3) of the EEC Treaty and Article 108(3) of the Euratom Treaty, yet enthusiasm for this was muted compared with the rhetoric of the Ad Hoc Assembly.

The Treaties of Rome granted the European Parliamentary Assembly a greater role in the legislative sphere than the Common Assembly had enjoyed. Rather than just 'supervisory' powers, the reconstituted Assembly was to have 'advisory' powers under Article 7 of the EEC Treaty. However, the Commission's role had declined in comparison with that of the ECSC High Authority, rendering the Assembly's new powers rather insignificant. Thus, once again, the treaty as ratified paid little attention to the parliamentary dimension of the European project.

Conclusions

The prevailing approach in the early years of the integration process was that favoured by Monnet and Schuman: integration in stages and an incremental shift towards federalism. The result was the creation of a set of institutions which tied together a number of states in a quasi-federal structure within which certain powers were delegated to a supranational authority. Thus the federalists seemed to have achieved some of the institutions they desired, although on a rather limited basis and as a result of the need for the supranational High Authority to be democratically accountable rather than for exclusively idealistic reasons. They did not accomplish a 'great leap forward' towards a federal Europe. The integration process could therefore be seen as the triumph of pragmatism over idealism.

Naturally there were dissenters who did not support moves towards a federal Europe and who were reluctant to accept any delegation of sovereignty to a supranational authority, even one subject to the scrutiny of a parliamentary assembly. Such views were held by the majority of the political elites in Britain and the Scandinavian countries, who refused to follow the federalist path. While in the late 1940s and early 1950s these views were held by only a minority in the six founding EC states, as the next chapter indicates, they came to dominate the integration process when General de Gaulle was President of France.

In the 1950s, however, it was left to Michel Debré (one of those who favoured cooperation between nation states rather than peoples) to raise one question which was not seriously addressed by anyone else in either the Ad Hoc Assembly or the Spaak Committee: how legitimate a mandate would the European Parliament have? The implicit assumption running through Article 38 of the EDC Treaty, the resolution of the Consultative Assembly, the Luxembourg Resolution and the work of the Ad Hoc Assembly was that a federal Europe founded on democratic principles was possible; the only remaining question was: how best could it be constituted?

For Debré these views were not so obvious. In his opinion direct elections would not be sufficient to validate the powers the proposed parliament would wield. 'It is easy to set up a parliament, but one looks in vain for its authority...in political life there are only national realities in Europe...a European state could only be created by force...neither the American nor the German example is valid for Europe' (Ad Hoc Assembly, 1952f: 10 [my translation]). This idea is vital: if Debré was right and elections alone do not confer the legitimacy that the proponents of a federal Europe based on democratic principles claim, one might question the sense of having a supranational parliament at all. The validity of Debré's scepticism, and its implications, will be considered in subsequent chapters.

3 |

From Appointed Assembly to Direct Elections and Beyond

The Treaty of Paris had permitted direct elections to the Common Assembly; the Treaties of Rome actually required such elections to the single Assembly which was to serve the three European Communities. Moreover, whereas the Treaty of Paris envisaged elections being held in accordance with national provisions, Article 138(3) of the Treaty establishing the EEC and Article 108(3) of the Treaty establishing the European Atomic Energy Community demanded that they be held under a common electoral system:

> The Assembly shall draw up proposals for elections by direct universal suffrage in accordance with a uniform procedure in all member states.
>
> The Council shall, acting unanimously, lay down the appropriate provisions, which it shall recommend to the Member States for adoption in accordance with their respective constitutional requirements.[1]

The decision that the Assembly should make proposals for direct elections was taken because of anxiety that if the proposals were made in the Treaty framework itself, national parliaments might have refused to ratify the Treaties at all (Gerbet 1992: 15).

A period of twenty-two years elapsed between the signing of the Treaties of Rome and the introduction of the direct elections to the European Parliament which they required. This period was marked by attempts by the Parliament to bring about elections and by the Council of Ministers' reluctance to act. Why did the necessary legislation take so long and what eventually allowed the introduction of direct elections?

This chapter examines the issues and controversies surrounding the idea of direct elections. It looks at why direct elections were seen as

---

1.   As discussed in Chapter 5, this provision was revised slightly by the Treaty of Amsterdam (Article 190 TEC).

necessary or desirable and assesses the merits of certain frequent assertions concerning the nature of a directly elected assembly. Four recur-
ring themes will be considered: first, the assumptions concerning the
nature of representation above the level of the nation state and the existence (actual or potential) of a European public opinion; secondly, the
practical problems of introducing a common electoral system which
emerged in the process of drafting the Dehousse Report; thirdly, the
nature of the powers that such an elected assembly would wield;
fourthly, and related to the previous point, the reluctance of national
politicians to accept a shift in the locus of decision-making to the
European level. This last problem emerged most forcefully with
President de Gaulle's antipathy to any sort of federal Europe, and highlights a continuing tension between those who favour some form of
federal Europe and those who insist on intergovernmental cooperation.
Both sides viewed direct elections as a federalist symbol; the difference
came in the value they placed on such a symbol.

One feature of the debate over the postwar years was a gradual shift
away from the optimistic belief held by the proponents of European
integration that 'the peoples' supported this process. Thus, the rhetoric
changed as the supporters of elections placed less emphasis on their
value for mobilizing existing popular support for European integration
and began to argue that elections would serve as a way of creating
necessary popular support for further integration.

The prospect of direct elections had been raised at the Congress of
The Hague, since most of those present at the Congress were federalists
and, as Emile Noël pointed out, 'The achievement of an assembly
directly elected by the people is clearly the *sine qua non* of a genuine
European federation' (Congress of Europe at The Hague 1948a: 15d).
However, calls for immediate elections were muted, since even those
who were, in principle, in favour of them felt that there should be a
delay until national governments and parliaments were ready.

Fundamental to many of the demands for direct elections which
emerged at the Congress and persisted in subsequent negotiations, were
the belief that the European Communities must be 'democratic' and the
associated assumption that the Parliament and direct elections to it
would provide that democratic element. Subsequent debate at the time
of the Schuman Plan envisaged a separation of powers as the model for
the European Coal and Steel Community, itself predicated on the idea
that the Community could possess the features of a democracy.

Thus, for many, the view that direct elections would give the Communities a necessary democratic dimension demonstrated underlying federalist assumptions about European integration, a sign that the Community was not merely a technocratic enterprise (Herman and Lodge 1978: 1). Yet this argument was accepted even by those who were opposed to the idea of a European state. For example in 1976, Margaret Thatcher, then leader of the Conservative Party in opposition, stated:

> The Conservative Party...supports direct elections... I would not myself support direct elections if I felt that they would undermine the traditional role of the House of Commons. But the truth is that there is a different task to be done, which we believe should have a democratic institution (cited in Jackson 1993: 191).

Former President of the Commission, Walter Hallstein, viewed elections in a more positive light, commenting that:

> In a democracy the system of government rests entirely on the authority of its people, its citizens: 'The power of the state is derived from the people.' And the channel for this in the European Community is the Parliament, which represents the people (Hallstein 1972: 73).

Hallstein's words imply that for him at least the European Community could be seen as a state, albeit one which lacked many of the institutional features of other democratic states.

This line of argument highlights an important difference between the EC and more traditional international organizations: no one raises the question of whether the United Nations is democratic; it is simply accepted as an intergovernmental organization which gives a limited role to national representatives in its assembly. Herman and Lodge have suggested that direct elections reflect a decision to turn the EC into federal entity:

> it has been recognized that direct elections hold the key to the future of the EC. They have been seen as confirming and defining the existence, nature and political form of the Community—as resolving its ontological problems in favour of federalism (1978: 1).

This opinion is useful in clarifying one view of elections, but is inadequate as it stands. When direct elections were finally introduced there was no clear convergence on the view that the EC should be a federal entity. Indeed, one could still assert, as the Dehousse Report of May 1960 (para. 27) had done, that, 'The entire structure of the Communities, in its present form, is not in line with our current ideas of political organization.' Arguably little had changed forty years later, despite repeated Treaty amendment. What, then, did the founders hope to achieve with the introduction of direct elections? The following section outlines the functions elections are usually held to serve, before considering the arguments surrounding direct elections to the EP.

The Functions of Elections

> ...people vote in elections, people concern themselves with the result of elections, when they see some purpose to the use of their votes; and this Assembly has not given evidence of that kind to the peoples of Europe (Gwyneth Dunwoody cited in Jackson 1993: 192).

This indictment of the European Parliament was made in the European Parliament prior to direct elections by the British Labour MP, Gwyneth Dunwoody, at that time also an MEP. The justification for her accusations can only be understood by a comparison with elections at the national level.

Elections are used to fill certain official positions. One major function of elections whether in parliamentary, presidential or semi-presidential systems, is *government formation.* In most West European states—France being the major exception—the executive emerges from the legislature and is dependent on it to be able to govern effectively. Even in those countries where the legislative and executive are separate, the executive is typically dependent on the parliamentary majority, so the election results have a significant impact on government.[2] National elections typically play an important role in the political life of a state, even if the institution elected is not particularly powerful in its own right. Thus, for example, the British general election matters not because the House of Commons is powerful, but rather because the outcome of the elections determines who governs.

In the United States, where the separation of powers doctrine means that the President is independent of Congress, the Congressional elections have no impact on government formation. However, like elections in most Western European states, they do have a major impact on

---

2.   The French position is somewhat different since the President enjoys individual legitimacy by virtue of direct election. However, from the mid-1980s periods of 'cohabitation' have shown the importance of legislative elections, which can act as a curb on presidential power.

public policy formation—or lawmaking—since Congress enjoys the right of legislative initiative. Moreover, people tend to identify with 'their' representative in Congress because of the benefits they can provide, for example delivering government contracts to the district and intervening in the Federal Administration on behalf of their constituents.

A final function of elections is the 'legitimation of power' (Beetham 1991). The assumption here is that by casting a vote electors are expressing their support for a political regime. Mackenzie has even suggested that:

> If one had to ground the defense of elections on a single maxim it would doubtless be that of the Puritan revolution: 'There are no laws that in their strictness and vigour of justice any man is bound to that are not made by those whom he doth consent to' (1968: 6).

What role were European elections expected to perform? And do they perform that role? How far do they contribute to government formation or to public policy formation or to regime support?

Deliberations at the Congress of The Hague and the Ad Hoc Assembly: Reprise

The Congress of The Hague

There was little doubt in the minds of those present at the Congress of The Hague that the citizens broadly supported close European cooperation, or integration. Indeed, as noted in the previous chapter, there was even a feeling that public opinion might be ahead of governments, with Belgian Prime Minister and Foreign Minister, Paul-Henri Spaak, proposing that the peoples should urge their governments to act.

Despite the assumption of popular support, however, there was little complacency. In his draft memorandum prior to the Congress, Duncan Sandys (1947: 2) said that the Political Report should 'announce the launching of an intensive international campaign to secure the sympathy and support of public opinion without which effective Government action will be impossible'.

Paul Reynaud called for immediate direct elections to a European consultative assembly, in the belief that:

> it is only possible to stir up public opinion in our different countries and to overcome national egoism by making an appeal to a new sovereignty which can only spring from universal European suffrage (Reynaud 1948:32a).

Admittedly this proposal was not for a European Parliament, but for a weaker consultative assembly. Ultimately the limited scope of the assembly's powers contributed to the delegates' rejection of the idea of direct elections in the short term even though many favoured such elections in the longer term.

Support for direct elections was echoed in many quarters. By virtue of elections themselves, Coudenhove-Kalergi (1948) believed, the assembly would wield significant moral authority which governments would not easily be able to override. Conversely the likelihood of a directly elected parliament acquiring such authority was another reason why the final resolution did not support elections; as Macmillan argued:

> I should be very much surprised if any of the Governments or any of the European Parliaments would in fact introduce legislation, and pass it by the end of the year, which introduced a system of a European Parliament to be elected upon this basis (Congress of Europe 1948a: 14).

Although some delegates foresaw a sense of European identity replacing national identities, this was seen as too radical even for a committed federalist like Henrik Brugmans. He argued that a federal state must respect local and regional communities and the idea of one representative for every million *European* citizens would violate this principle (Congress of Europe 1948a: 16d). As a Dutchman, Brugmans might well have been reluctant to contemplate the prospect of Benelux representatives being dominated by the large number of French and German representatives.

Others foresaw no difficulties in creating a European public opinion. Convinced as they were of popular support for European integration, they believed that a directly elected assembly was the appropriate mechanism to mobilize such opinion. In the context of federalist aspirations, therefore, it was felt that the sovereignties which nation states must cede to the European level should pass to the assembly—a line of argument prefiguring solutions to later claims of a 'democratic deficit' in European decision-making.

Objections to direct elections came from pragmatists as much as from those who objected to the whole enterprise. The nation state loomed large and there was a danger, as Macmillan pointed out, that excessive demands could result in national governments being reluctant to act. Such arguments won the day in 1948, but were challenged again in the Ad Hoc Assembly between 1952 and 1954.

The Ad Hoc Assembly
By contrast, there was little dispute in the Ad Hoc Assembly about the creation of an assembly for the envisaged Political Community, nor that it should be democratically elected.[3] The assumption that some form of supranational democracy was feasible was still made but, as at the Congress of The Hague, there were disagreements over the desirability of direct elections for the proposed legislative assembly. As Fernand Dehousse pointed out, the democratic dimension was required by Article 38 of the EDC Treaty, while the requirements for such democracy were not made clear (Ad Hoc Assembly 1952c: 12).

A case for early elections was that only an assembly subject to popular suffrage would have the political authority necessary to be the recipient of the sovereignties that would be lost by nation states under the provisions of a European Political Community. The widespread assumption was that direct elections would confer democratic legitimacy on the process of European integration and on the assembly in particular. There was also a feeling that elections would help foster a sense of common identity and popular support for the enterprise, and were thus the precondition for a political community.

There were some dissenters from this position. Debré, for example, questioned the authority of a directly elected assembly since, he claimed, there was no European political identity (Ad Hoc Assembly 1952f: 10-11). The Dutch delegation was also reluctant to accept direct elections, at least in the short term, because they felt they could bring destructive elements into the assembly and also because there were no European political parties or programmes (Ad Hoc Assembly 1952e: 9-10).[4]

Debré, who opposed the concept of direct elections, suggested a pan-European referendum to ratify his proposals for a pact of European nations. Debré's approach was a classic Gaullist one rejecting the idea of indirect representation via political parties and preferring to let the 'people' speak directly by means of referendums, the instrument favoured by de Gaulle himself, both in French and European politics.

3.   This section draws on material from the Ad Hoc Assembly papers located in the European Communities Archives held at the European University Institute in Florence.
4.   This raises the question of whether political parties and programmes can be expected to emerge prior to the establishment of a polity in which they operate.

Thus even those who rejected the introduction of direct elections did not necessarily reject the idea that there should be some form of transnational democracy. However, they refused to accept the idea that transnational *institutions* might have some form of legitimacy, which they argued resided exclusively in the nation state.

Although the Ad Hoc Assembly's proposals collapsed with the demise of the EDC, the ideal of direct elections continued through the Messina Conference and the negotiations in the Spaak Committee, culminating in the Treaties of Rome in 1957 which made explicit provision for elections in the form of Article 138(3) of the EEC Treaty and Article 108(3) of the Euratom Treaty.

From Dehousse and Patijn to Direct Election

Members of the European Parliament acted quickly to fulfil their new treaty obligation to propose legislation for elections by 'direct universal suffrage'. A Working Party chaired by Fernand Dehousse was set up to study the issue in October 1958, only 18 months after the signing of the Treaties of Rome. In addition to the general report, known as the Dehousse Report, reports were produced by Mr Faure on the 'composition of the elected Parliament' and by Mr Schuijt on 'questions relating to the electoral system of the Parliament to be elected', which served as Explanatory Statements to Chapter 1 and to Chapters 2 and 3 respectively of the main report. The Report was adopted by the Parliament in May 1960.

The political significance of the proposed elections was taken as given by the Working Party. Whereas the prevailing opinion at the Congress of The Hague had been that the public broadly supported European integration, by the late 1950s the argument had shifted. Thus the Working Party argued that:

> What is largely wanting in the European Communities has already been stressed by others: popular support, recognition by the European peoples of their solidarity, the shared realization that a national framework is constrictive and that it is in the Communities alone that Europe can look forward to any sort of future (Dehousse Report 1960: para. 24).

This situation had arisen because of the prevalence of technocratic experts in the Communities, something the Working Party strongly opposed. 'It is high time, therefore, that the peoples be drawn into this venture, and that they grasp what is at stake and the attendant risks, and make known their will' (Dehousse Report 1960: para. 24). This led the Working Party to the conclusion that elections were necessary since:

> under various forms, we know and practise but a single method of expressing the will of the people and of associating them with the management of public affairs—free elections (Dehousse Report 1960: para. 25).

For their supporters, direct elections were therefore seen as a means both to engender the popular support necessary for the success of European integration and also to permit expression of the 'popular will'. This view was contested by those who favoured plebiscitary rather than representative democracy, not least because of the problem of whether political parties which typically fight elections allow any meaningful expression of will.[5]

Despite broad support in the Committee for elections, agreement on practical matters was far less easy to achieve. Problems arose concerning, *inter alia*, the nature of the electoral system, links with national parliaments, the number of members and the transitional arrangements. In particular, there were questions concerning the nature of the electoral system to be used. The Treaty called for a 'uniform procedure', a requirement which was seen to go beyond a 'purely technical matter' to a matter of principle concerning the relative merits of proportional and majoritarian electoral systems (Schuijt Report 1960: para. 2). The former seemed most appropriate for reflecting public opinion; the latter for electing a Parliament capable of producing a strong, homogeneous government. More specifically, electoral practices varied considerably between the Member States, leading to a situation where, 'Although most of the politicians consulted favoured the same electoral system for all six States, they were not slow to add that they could only accept a uniform system if it were broadly in line with their own' (Schuijt Report 1960: para. 8). Five of the six Member States used some form of proportional representation (France with its two ballot majoritarian system was the exception), but the details of the systems differed enormously.

The final proposal (Dehousse Report 1960: para. 18) was a compro-

---

5.   The 1992 Maastricht referendum in France produced a further twist to this set of arguments: ostensibly a referendum on the issue of the ratification of the Treaty on European Union, it became a contest between supporters and opponents of President Mitterrand.

mise, allowing each Member State to devise its own electoral rules for the first direct elections, since the Working Party judged that 'uniformity was not synonymous with identity'. Thus, provided the states all adopted laws in accordance with certain common principles aimed at ensuring 'universal, free, equal and secret elections', they would be deemed to be following a uniform system and fulfilling the terms of the Treaty. Nevertheless, the Working Party did not take this to be a definitive solution, leaving it to the directly elected Parliament to devise a 'uniform electoral law…at the end of a *transitional* period'.

Members of the Working Party were also mindful of the need for support from national parliaments since:

> European integration is only beginning. Major decisions are being taken, and will long continue to be, by the national Governments set up and controlled by the Parliaments. It is in the latter, as Minister von Merkatz pointed out in Bonn, that the process of political integration will take place (Faure Report 1960: para. 8).

Thus it was proposed that only two-thirds of the Members of the European Parliament should be directly elected, the other third being nominated by national parliaments. This would serve to maintain links between national and European parliaments and also 'to dispel any mistrust the national Parliaments might feel of an elected European Parliament' (Faure Report 1960: para. 9).

The Council of Ministers did not show such enthusiasm for direct elections. In particular, the rise to power in France of Charles de Gaulle had rendered unthinkable moves which could be construed as leading to a federal Europe. De Gaulle's approach only permitted cooperation between sovereign nation states and he refused to countenance the legitimacy of supranational elements of European integration.[6] Thus, the Council did not respond to the draft Convention nor to subsequent parliamentary demands that it fulfil its treaty obligations. For example the 1963 Furler Report on the competences and powers of the EP urged the Council to act on the draft Convention, arguing that failure to do so had already caused delays in the process of unification.

On 12 March 1969, the European Parliament finally issued an ultimatum to the Council that if it did not adopt the draft Convention the

---

6.   Indeed, one of de Gaulle's reasons for initiating the 'crisis of the empty chair' in 1965 was his opposition to the idea that the European Parliament should be granted more powers.

Parliament would bring a case before the Court of Justice. The resignation of de Gaulle only months later unblocked the deadlock in the Council. The new French President, Pompidou, was willing to compromise with EC partners in a package deal with mutual concessions aimed at relaunching the Community. The relaunch paved the way for enlargement negotiations, which necessitated a reassessment of the existing institutional arrangements, and some progress towards direct elections could finally be made. While not actually giving any firm guarantees, the Heads of State and Government announced at the conclusion of The Hague Summit in December 1969 that 'The problem of direct elections will continue to be studied by the Council of Ministers' (Heads of State or Government 1970: para. 5). Even this shift did not reflect a clear commitment to direct elections, however.

Parliament again tried to make the Council act in 1970, and finally took the initiative itself, beginning to draw up new proposals for direct elections, based on the Dehousse Report, with Schelto Patijn as *rapporteur*. Only in 1974 when France elected a non-Gaullist President, Valéry Giscard d'Estaing, did the Heads of State or Government finally decide as part of a new package deal that the time had come to act on their treaty obligation and even to set a date for the first elections. By this time, the Parliament was already close to completing its revised proposals, which were adopted in the form of the Patijn Report on 14 January 1975.

There was little difference between the Dehousse and Patijn Reports except that the latter did not allow for any delegated MEPs who were no longer deemed necessary to placate national MPs. There was no discernible shift towards a uniform electoral system; it was left to the European Parliament to devise one.

The decision to introduce direct elections came during a period of stagnation for the EC following the 1973 energy crisis and in part reflected the approach of the incoming French President, Giscard, who felt that direct elections would encourage political dynamism (Tindemans 1994). The economic difficulties contributed to an apparent loss of public support for European integration, as national problems prevailed. Thus at the same time as proposals were being made for Article 138 of the Treaty of Rome to be fulfilled, at the December 1974 Paris Summit, the Heads of State and Government also asked one of their number, the Belgian Prime Minister, Leo Tindemans, to produce a report on European Union looking at ways of generating renewed public support. Noting the apparent decline of popular support for the European ideal, Tindemans argued:

> No one wants to see a technocratic Europe. European Union must be experienced by the citizen in his daily life... It must protect the rights of the individual and strengthen democracy through a set of institutions which have legitimacy conferred upon them by the will of our peoples (Tindemans Report 1976: Section VI).

Elections were now perceived by some members of the Council as contributing a necessary democratic component to the European enterprise. Moreover, Tindemans viewed elections as a way of eliciting the public support he deemed vital for the success of European integration.[7] Indeed, he claims that when the decision was finally taken to introduce direct elections:

> All European leaders at that moment were convinced that what we needed was to convince public opinion. The best method was to organize direct elections so that the political parties would be forced to put the proposals and how they conceived Europe and explain in understandable language what Europe meant (Tindemans 1994).

Likewise, the then Commission President, François-Xavier Ortoli, told the European Parliament that direct elections were an important means of bringing about 'the involvement of public opinion in the construction of Europe' (Ortoli 1975) . Thus it was hoped that direct elections would boost the integration process. More fundamentally it was an important symbolic step in the quest to 'build up the new European institutional system in accordance with democratic principles' (Ortoli 1975).

Parliamentary Power and Direct Elections

Direct elections were not only intended to make the integration process more legitimate, they were closely tied to debates about the EP's powers. From the outset there was an implicit assumption that the powers, or at any rate influence and prestige, of the Parliament would be increased as a result of direct elections (Herman and Lodge 1978: 4-5).

---

7.   This public support was not considered so important by some, for example, Monnet who favoured a technocratic Europe devoid of 'political activity'. The tragedy for Tindemans was that 'Europe was never a mass movement' (Tindemans 1994).

The close relationship between powers and elections was deliberately played down by supporters of direct elections, precisely because of the danger that national parliamentarians, jealously guarding their own powers, might reject elections if they thought their positions would be weakened. Thus, while the Dehousse Report noted:

> The position of the Working Party is quite clear. The connection between elections and the powers of the Parliament is too obvious to need underlining. If elections are to make any sense at all they must endow the Parliament, through direct investiture, with a legitimacy and strength from which it will draw political power (1960: para. 28).

The first draft Convention avoided making such links too explicit, since the Working Party:

> feared that the introduction of direct elections might be threatened if too close a link were to be forced between direct elections and the question of powers (Dehousse Report 1960: para. 55).

Such elections would, it was assumed, endow the EP with a certain legitimacy, and hence moral authority, which had formerly been the exclusive right of national parliaments.[8] However, individual protagonists had different implicit and explicit objectives; agreement on direct elections arose from a coalition of pragmatists, moderate integrationists and federalists.

Even before the introduction of direct elections, parliamentarians pressed for increased powers on the grounds that they were the representatives of the peoples and were vested with a democratic legitimacy in a way that the other EC institutions were not, by virtue of being elected, albeit at the national level. As the EC's sphere of influence grew, so anxiety arose about the loss of accountability in European decision-making, leading moderate integrationists and pragmatists to accept the need for the elections which federalists held so dear. The problem of powers shifting from the national level, where they were subject to parliamentary scrutiny, to the European level where they were taken by members of national executives acting as the legislative body, with inadequate scrutiny—later known as the 'democratic deficit'—had thus been raised as early as 1962.

In his report on the evolution of Community institutions, Charles Janssens (1963) had argued that the Commission should be subject to a

---

8.   For a discussion and critique of the conventional arguments see Herman and Lodge (1978: Chapter 6).

parliamentary vote of confidence. Yet he was also concerned that unless the Councils began to take some notice of the Parliament's opinions a situation would arise where EC legislation, which was increasingly replacing national legislation, would not be decided by a parliamentary body, but by the Council of Ministers, which was not accountable to either national parliaments or the European Parliament. In the long run, Janssens asserted, this would have 'unfortunate consequences for the democratic structure of the Community' (Janssens Report 1960: para. 8 [my translation]). Janssens thus concluded that the European Parliament should be granted a larger say in the legislative process, even before the introduction of direct elections.

After a lapse of several years during which the Council declined to act on direct elections in spite of the more favourable rhetoric of the 1969 Hague Summit Communiqué, the Parliament set up a working group chaired by Professor Georges Vedel. The eponymous Vedel Report produced in 1972 recognized the interrelation between elections and parliamentary powers, addressing the circular problem of whether one could realistically have elections to a weak institution or whether it was necessary first to increase its powers, in turn raising the question of whether it was feasible to give additional powers to an unelected body. Like Janssens, the Working Group rejected the idea that elections must precede the extension of powers, since:

> in this way, two equally desirable objectives are making each other's implementation impossible. The only way to break the vicious circle is to refuse to let one of the two objectives depend on the achievement of the other one first (Vedel Report 1972: 59).

The Vedel Report concluded that powers should be increased even if direct elections were not introduced in the short term. The powers granted to the EP in the budgetary sphere in 1970 following the introduction of Community 'own resources' could be argued to have created a precedent for enlarging parliamentary powers without any shifts towards elections.[9] Although the counter argument can be made that

---

9.   Prior to 1970 the EC was financed by contributions from the Member States. The 1969 Summit of Heads of State or Government took the decision that the EC should have its own resources. Since these funds would belong to the Community, national parliaments could not oversee the use of these resources and so the Commission proposed an amendment to Article 201 of the EEC Treaty to increase the EP's powers and, hence, offer a European-level mechanism for overseeing these funds.

there should be 'No taxation without representation', and that the MEPs could not be considered as true representatives if they were not elected, the MEPs used the tactical argument that as the power of the Parliament increased, so the enhanced prestige it enjoyed would make it easier to convince national MPs to work for direct elections.

The case of budgetary powers is important since it highlights the view that even an indirectly elected assembly was the appropriate organ to endow the EC with greater democratic accountability (Wallace 1979b: 286). Elections were not seen to be vital to the role of the Assembly; they were, however, seen as desirable for the democratic legitimacy that they would confer on the Assembly and indirectly on the EC. By virtue of this legitimation, the Assembly would then enjoy increased influence and have an enhanced claim on further powers, or so it was argued. While parliamentarians were at the forefront of such arguments, Leo Tindemans, at that time Belgian Prime Minister, also declared that:

> Direct elections to the Parliament will give this Assembly a new political authority. At the same time it will reinforce the democratic legitimacy of the whole European institutional apparatus (Tindemans Report 1976: Section V, A).

The assumption underpinning the argument of the smaller member governments, at least concerning the European Union and its institutions, was that they should be democratically accountable. Elections were the best way of ensuring compensation for any loss of democratic accountability caused by the process of European integration. The indirectly elected Assembly had some claims to legitimacy since its members were elected at the *national* level, but this was increasingly inadequate as the European Community gained new powers.

When the European Parliament was first elected in 1979, its Members were quick to press for increased powers, as well as to express their willingness to make the maximum use of existing powers, claiming that the elections did indeed give them a greater legitimacy. Immediately after the first elections in May 1979, parliamentarians made use of their right to veto the Community Budget for the first time, in large part as a way of demonstrating their increased importance. Subsequently they fought for further powers, arguing, as they had done in the 1972 Vedel Report, that as competences shifted to the European Community, out of the control of national parliaments, decisions were being made without effective parliamentary supervision.

The directly-elected Parliament's next major attempt to demonstrate its new-found role came in the form of a 'Draft Treaty Establishing European Union'—the Spinelli Report. Adopted by the Parliament in February 1984, the Draft Treaty emerged from the Ad Hoc Committee on Institutional Affairs that had been set up in the wake of direct elections, and owed its creation to the veteran advocate of a federal Europe, Altiero Spinelli (see Cardozo and Corbett 1985). The Spinelli Report provided a *de facto* blueprint for a federal Europe based on the principles of parliamentary democracy and offered the EC the outline of a fully formed constitution. The MEPs' demands were not met at that time but, as the following chapter shows, the powers of the European Parliament did expand in the twenty years following the introduction of direct elections. The increased powers were granted partly as a result of the directly-elected Parliament's enhanced claims to legitimacy, but have to be seen in the context of desires to increase Community competences more generally, which necessitated revised decision-making procedures.

One area where MEPs made less progress was in devising a uniform electoral system, although by 1999 it seemed that there was at least some chance of securing a system based on common, albeit not identical, principles. Member States were allowed to adopt their own electoral rules for the first European elections, as long as they were based on certain 'fundamental principles of democratic elections, ie. elections must be equal, free, universal, direct and secret' (Patijn Report 1974: Article 7). It was thus left to the elected EP to propose a common system. By 1994, three serious attempts to devise a common system had come to naught.[10] The Seitlinger Report was passed by the EP in March 1982, but did not get through the Council of Ministers. The subsequent Bocklet draft was shelved by the Parliament in 1985, when it became clear that agreement on a common system could not be found. Progress was finally made on 10 March 1993, when the EP passed the De Gucht Report. However, the Report was still awaiting consideration by the Council of Ministers at the time of the 1994 elections, which were consequently fought under the old rules: in 1989 and 1994 this meant that the elections were fought under 13 different sets of electoral regulations, including two in the United Kingdom.

---

10. For further details of the various attempts to devise a common electoral system, see Anastassopoulos (1998).

Some progress towards a more uniform electoral system was made at the Amsterdam Summit. The ensuing Treaty of Amsterdam revised Article 138(3) (Article 190 TEC) to read:

> The European Parliament shall draw up a proposal for elections by direct universal suffrage in accordance with a uniform procedure in all Member States or in accordance with principles common to all Member States.

Although the revised Article did not impose the requirement of uniformity, it represented an advance on the previous situation, since it seemed to imply that the new British government under Tony Blair might be willing to concede the principle of proportional representation—the only electoral principle that was not common to all the Member States (Duff 1997: 150-51). Following a major battle with the hereditary peers in the House of Lords, which almost derailed its proposed legislation for changing the electoral procedure for European elections, the government invoked the Parliament Act, which enabled them to override the Lords' opposition. This paved the way for the introduction of a system of closed regional list proportional representation for the 1999 elections.

Conclusions and Questions Arising in the 1990s

The general thrust of elite opinion accepted the conventional wisdom that elections could and do confer democratic legitimacy on the institutions of the European Union. It was also assumed that the elections would help to arouse that public support for European integration deemed necessary for its success. De Gaulle was not alone in questioning the feasibility of creating a European federation and the democratic credentials of the EC in the 1960s, but a majority of EC governments were receptive to arguments for democratic legitimacy at the European level.[11]

By the late 1980s, however, the situation seemed to have altered: national parliaments had increased their cooperative links with the European Parliament, leading to the 'assizes'—a Conference of the European Parliament and national parliaments which met in Rome in

---

11. When 'asked who or what could unite Europe within a federation', at a press conference on 15 May 1962, de Gaulle 'came to the conclusion that no-one possessed sufficient power, standing or ability to achieve it' (Schöndube 1992: 37).

November 1990 in the run-up to the Maastricht Treaty Intergovernmental Conference. Whereas during the early years of European integration the European Parliament had attempted to act as the sole representative of the peoples of Europe, by 1990 it recognized the need for support from national parliaments. Similarly, in its contribution to the Maastricht Treaty Intergovernmental Conference, the Commission asserted:

> Further democratization of the running of the Community must be seen from the twin standpoint of its institutions and its citizens.
> (1) Without losing sight of the paramount need to reconcile democracy and efficiency, the objective as far as the institutions are concerned must be twofold:
>   (a) to strengthen the powers of the European Parliament:
>   (b) to increase the involvement of national parliaments (cited in European Parliament 1992b: 63).

Additionally, the 1993 decision of the German Constitutional Court in relation to the Maastricht Treaty stressed the continued dominance of national parliaments, arguing that democratic legitimation of European integration came primarily from national parliaments. The Court did, however, accept:

> a growing need for the democratic legitimation and influence channeled through the national parliaments to be 'seconded' by representation of the nations by a European Parliament, which afforded 'additional' democratic support for the policies of the European Union (Research Services of the German Federal Parliament 1993).

Coupled with occasional calls by national politicians, including the British Foreign Secretary, Robin Cook, for a second chamber of national parliamentarians, this seemed to indicate a possible renationalization, or continuing national dominance, of politics. Many of the assumptions underpinning the introduction of direct elections had thus come into question. National parliaments were still seen by most as the basis for giving the European enterprise legitimacy. Nevertheless, the European Parliament's powers and influence continued to increase and although the Treaty of Amsterdam contains a Protocol on the Role of National Parliaments in the European Union, which seeks to 'encourage greater involvement of national parliaments in the activities of the European Union' (cited in European Parliament 1998c: 9), it does not indicate a resurgence of national parliaments at the expense of the European Parliament's powers.

4 |

The European Parliament: A Subordinate Institution?

> They are called 'parliaments'—places where talk is carried on, 'talking shops' in the opinion of their critics. They are called 'congresses' or 'assemblies'. They are composed of houses of representatives, houses of the people, chambers of deputies, and senates (Wheare 1963: 1).

The European Parliament began life as a consultative assembly, endowed with relatively few powers. Over the years its influence and substantive powers have increased, yet the perception of the EP as a weak institution has persisted. Comparison with national parliaments in Western Europe suggests that the EP of 1999 is not a particularly weak institution. In many policy areas the EP could be seen to have considerably more power and influence than many national parliaments.

National Legislatures in Perspective

> Every traveller who, curious in political affairs, enquires in the countries which he visits how their legislative bodies are working, receives from the elder men the same discouraging answer. They tell him, in terms much the same everywhere, that there is less brilliant speaking than in the days of their own youth, that the tone of manners has declined, that the best citizens are less disposed to enter the chamber, that its proceedings are less fully reported and excite less interest, that a seat in it confers less social status, and that, for one reason or another, the respect felt for it has waned (Bryce 1921: 47).

Lord Bryce's words refer to the situation at the beginning of the twentieth century, yet are equally applicable to national parliaments in the 1990s. Over the decades, national legislatures have frequently been seen to have declined in importance as a result of the rise of mass democracy, the introduction of universal suffrage, the related rise of political parties and also executive dominance (Loewenberg 1971b: 3-

13). If national legislatures have declined since some 'golden age' of parliaments, should elections to the European Parliament be assessed against criteria that no longer fully apply to national elections? What are the functions of legislatures in the late twentieth century?

There are many different types of legislature, some powerful, many weak. Their roles differ considerably in various national political systems, depending on whether the systems are, for example, parliamentary, presidential or semi-presidential and on the specific constitutional rules in force. Drawing on the work of Walter Bagehot (1963:151-54) and others, the functions of a parliament can be taken to be: legislative; representative; financial; control; elective; informative; and supportive.[1]

Writing in 1867, Bagehot believed the 'elective'—the choice of who should govern—to be the most important function of the House of Commons. In an age before the extension of the franchise and the growth of political parties the individual MP's role in this activity was much greater than that of MPs in West European legislatures in the late twentieth century, who are constrained by their parties to act in a certain way. In effect, the elective function has been transferred to the voters themselves in two-party systems: the leader of the largest party becomes the head of government. In multi-party systems the formation of governments is still largely conducted through negotiations among parties, usually after the elections. Similarly, while parliamentarians may still express the will of their electors, voters frequently seek alternative ways of articulating desires or opinions, for example via the media or large pressure groups which can lobby governments more effectively than individual citizens or lone MPs (Wheare 1963: 228-34). The informative function is also shared, traditionally with the print media, but increasingly also with televisual and radio media (Wheare 1963: 227-28).

The rise of political parties and the increasingly important role played by the various media mean that national parliaments in Western Europe cannot all claim to fulfil Bagehot's functions. This could partly reflect the fact that the 'golden age' of legislatures, implied by those such as Bryce who argue that there has been a decline in the powers of

---

1.   For further discussion of the role of parliaments, see Bagehot (1963); von Beyme cited in Herman and Lodge (1978: 21-22); Wahlke (1971); and Packenham (1970).

legislatures, was somewhat mythical. However, it undoubtedly also reflects new constraints on parliamentarians which make it harder for them to act independently. In particular, the rise in executive power means that the role of legislatures has in many cases been reduced to supporting or moderating governmental initiatives. This is certainly the case in Britain and France. Furthermore, as Loewenberg (1971b: 12) points out, and as the referendums on the Maastricht Treaty suggested, increasing use of direct and plebiscitary democracy has also weakened the claims of parliaments to be the most accurate representatives of the citizens.

So much for the *functions* of parliaments, but how can we categorize the *nature* of parliaments? Michael Mezey (1979) has produced a typology of parliaments from across the world, which he ranks in terms of their policy-making power and how well supported they are. Considering the first variable, he asserts:

> Legislatures can be classified as possessing *strong policy-making power* if they can modify and reject executive proposals; legislatures that have no capacity to reject policy proposals but can modify them can be said to possess *moderate policy-making power*, while legislatures that can neither modify nor reject policy proposals have *little or no policy-making power* (Mezey 1979: 155-56).

As Philip Norton points out, a legislature must have the right of legislative *initiative* if it is to claim a strong policy-making function. Thus he suggests the following modifications to Mezey's definitions:

> ...Mezey's categories of 'strong' and 'modest': the first may be defined as the capacity to modify and reject policy as well as to substitute policy of one's own (policy-making); the second as the capacity to modify or reject but not to substitute policy of one's own (policy-influencing) (Norton 1990a: 5).

Norton's revision of Mezey's typology will be used as a framework for analysing the strength of the European Parliament.

The European Parliament in Comparative Perspective

The Treaties of Paris and Rome granted the European Parliament few powers: its legislative powers were constrained to the right of consultation and it was given no power of appointment. At the time of the first European elections, the EP was still weak, although its *de facto* functions were greater than its *de jure* powers, it had significant budgetary powers, and it did serve both an indirect representative function and an informative function (Herman and Lodge 1978: 16-17). Over the twenty years since the first direct elections, however, repeated treaty reforms have increased the EP's elective, control and legislative capacities, so that by 1999 the EP could be considered a 'moderate' legislature.

Elective Function
Initially, the Parliament had no choice over the composition of the European executive, that is the European Commissions/High Authority, which only became a single institution after the 1965 Merger Treaty. MEPs had no choice about the membership of the Commission, which was appointed by the Council of Ministers acting unanimously. An informal practice of MEPs giving a vote of confidence on the incoming Commission arose in the mid-1950s, when René Mayer made a speech to the Assembly, whose 'members gave their approval and claimed that it was a sort of approval procedure' (Gerbet 1992: 14-15). This was merely symbolic since the Council, which nominated the Commission, was not bound by the outcome of such votes. With the executive neither emerging from, nor chosen by, the Parliament, the EP effectively lacked an *elective* function.

Article 158 of the Maastricht Treaty (Article 214 TEC) gave the EP some influence over the composition of the Commission.

> The governments of the Member States shall nominate by common accord *after consulting the European Parliament*, the person they intend to appoint as President of the Commission.
>   ...The President and the other members of the Commission thus nominated shall be subject as a body to a vote of approval by the European Parliament.

The Treaty on European Union (TEU) only provides for Parliament to be *consulted* on the candidate for Commission President, but Members of the 1989–94 Parliament amended the EP's Rules of Procedure in order to maximize the effect of this power (European Parliament 1993). The Rules of Procedure (European Parliament 1998a: Rule 32, paras. 1 and 2) require the Commission President-designate to make a statement to a plenary session of Parliament, which then holds a vote of approval by roll-call. In fact, the President-designate in 1994 also made statements to, and answered questions from, the largest political groups prior to his statement to the plenary session. According to the Rules, in the event of a negative vote Parliament 'shall request the governments of the Member States to withdraw their proposal and present a new proposal to Parliament' (European Parliament 1998a: Rule 32, para. 4). Although their role at this stage is technically only advisory, MEPs felt that neither the individual candidate nor the Council would persist in a nomination that Parliament had rejected, an assumption given weight by the 1994 President-designate, Jacques Santer, who said he would not carry on if he did not win parliamentary support. In fact, the continued dominance of national politics, with national leaders warning their MEPs not to oppose Santer, meant that he won the parliamentary vote 260 votes in favour, 238 against and 23 abstentions, thus depriving the Parliament of the chance to use their new power to maximum effect (Smith 1995a: 75-76; Hix and Lord 1996).

MEPs also amended their Rules of Procedure to allow for congres-sional-style 'hearings' of individual Commissioners-designate prior to the vote on whole Commission (European Parliament 1998a: Rule 33). Thus, prior to the vote in plenary session, the Commissioners-designate were quizzed by an EP Committee according to the portfolio they were due to take up. Having decided to respect the principle of Commission collegiality, MEPs voted on the whole slate rather than individual can-didates. Changes introduced by the Treaty of Amsterdam effectively codify practices already adopted by the Parliament. Article 214 TEC thus provides for Parliament to be consulted formally on the Council's nominee for Commission President. It has been suggested by some, including former Commission President Jacques Delors, that European parties could indicate in advance of the elections their preferred candi-date for Commission President, in the event that their party family won a plurality of MEPs. If this situation were to come about, it would certainly offer electors some sense of being able to effect the composi-tion of the Commission; whether Member States would accept this scenario is another matter. The standard practice has been for the Commission to reflect the political balance in the Council rather than the Parliament. The nomination on 24 March 1999 of Italian former Prime Minister, Romano Prodi, a technocrat with social democratic leanings, to replace the disgraced Jacques Santer as President of the Commission initially seems to perpetuate that practice. However, it should be borne in mind that, unusually since the introduction of direct elections, the centre-left dominance in the Council was matched by that in the Parliament which was due to confirm Prodi in May 1999.

One key change under Amsterdam is that in future the Commission President-elect will be consulted over the composition of the incoming College of Commissioners. Since the EP will vote on the whole College, MEPs, or at least the heads of the largest groups, could perhaps exert influence on the political (and perhaps gender) balance of the nominees. Since the TEU brought the Commission's term in line with the parliamentary term, this would suggest that there will be considerable pressure for the Commission's political complexion to reflect that of the incoming parliament. This would be a significant shift from the traditional pattern whereby the Commission reflects the balance in Council and could have profound implications for EU decision-making, bearing in mind that the results of EP elections typically show an anti-government (and hence anti-Council) bias. As with the choice of Commission President, this scenario would require Member States to accept the shift; that is difficult to envisage, unless the parliamentary balance were such that MEPs could credibly threaten to block the incoming Commission. While the changes arising from the TEU and the Treaty of Amsterdam did not offer the Parliament the right to nominate Commissioners, they did mark a considerable advance towards an elective function and one which could be expressed to the voters in relatively simple terms, potentially giving them a greater interest in EP elections particularly in the wake of the events of March 1999.

In addition to its role in the appointment of the Commission, the European Parliament is consulted on the appointment of the Court of Auditors, the European Monetary Institute and the European Central Bank. The EP alone appoints the Ombudsman. The practice of parliamentary hearings was in fact begun in relation to the Court of Auditors (Westlake 1998: 432). In 1989, a negative vote by the Parliament on a nominee for the Court led France to withdraw its candidate, although the Greek Government refused to do likewise and their nominee was appointed. Moreover, in 1993 despite a negative EP vote on two of the Council's nominees, the Council still appointed all its preferred people, highlighting the limitations of the Parliament's powers in this regard (Westlake 1998: 433).

Control Functions
Article 24 of the ECSC Treaty, Article 144 of the EEC Treaty and Article 114 of the Euratom Treaty (Article 201 TEC) enabled the Parliament to dismiss the whole High Authority or Commission by a

two-thirds and absolute majority of MEPs, although the ECSC Treaty only gave the EP the right to censure the High Authority when the latter presented its annual report (Jacobs *et al.* 1992: 225). No provision was made for the dismissal of individual Commissioners. The agreement of the Commission to the EP's amended Rules of Procedure that Commissioners-designate should appear before a parliamentary committee, which would assess their competence and suitability, can be viewed as an extension of Parliament's powers of control, although no provision was made for the Parliament to vote on individual nominees. The Commission expressed hopes that the vote might increase its legitimacy, something that had frequently appeared to be lacking, as voters and politicians alike focused on this bureaucratic body when seeking to criticize European enterprises. Thus, for example, prior to the committee hearings, Marcelino Oreja, then a Commissioner-designate, declared in a written answer to the Institutional Affairs Committee that, 'From now on the European Parliament's approval will constitute its [the Commission's] main source of legitimacy' (Oreja 1994: 5 [my translation]). However, since repeated treaty reforms did not make any advance in terms of dismissing individual Commissioners, by 1999 it seemed the EP's power of censure remained a nuclear one, and hence seemed of limited use.[2] The resignation *en masse* of the Commission when the Committee of Independent Experts' Report was published did little to alter matters. Five Commissioners were named in the Report, yet the principle of Commission collegiality meant that they all had to resign.[3]

Aside from the formal right of censure, the founding treaties (Article 123 ECSC Treaty; Article 140 EEC Treaty; Article 110 Euratom Treaty) also required the European Commission to 'reply orally or in writing to questions put to it by the European Parliament or its Members', thus granting parliamentarians a weak *scrutinizing* or *control* function. This right was extended by the Maastricht Treaty to cover the areas of common foreign and security policy, and justice and

2.   For further discussion about the reluctance to censure individual Commissioners, see Westlake (1994b: 27).

3.   Had individual Commissioners, especially Edith Cresson and maybe Jacques Santer himself, 'volunteered' to resign immediately after publication of the Report, the situation may have been rather different. The whole episode put the idea of the right to censure individual Commissioners back on the EU agenda, possibly to be discussed at the next IGC, likely to occur in 2000.

home affairs (Maurer 1998: 28). The Parliament was not given the right to hold the Council of Ministers accountable for its activities, primarily because when the ECSC Assembly was established it was felt inappropriate for one parliamentary assembly to question the activities of another organ composed of ministers chosen by national parliaments (Gerbet 1992: 12). Gradually, however, the Council began to answer parliamentary questions and the practice was formalized in 1983 by Article 2.3.3 of the Solemn Declaration on European Union.

Commissioners also appear before EP committees to answer questions or make statements when draft Community legislation is being discussed (Jacobs *et al.* 1992: 121). This gives parliamentarians a stronger control function, as did a Treaty amendment of Article 149, para. 2b of the EEC Treaty, which requires the Council of Ministers to explain its decisions to the EP (Jacobs *et al.* 1992: 188-90). The EP's ability to exercise control was further increased by Article 138c of the TEU (Article 193 TEC) which gave the EP the right to convene temporary Committees of Inquiry to investigate 'alleged contraventions or maladministration in the implementation of Community law' (Maurer 1998: 29). Thus, in the wake of the British beef crisis, a Committee was set up on the BSE question, which gained some attention for the EP and, more importantly, contributed to changes in EU provisions on veterinary medicine under the Treaty of Amsterdam (Maurer 1998: 30). The case almost led to the Commission being censured, but in the end MEPs favoured a more limited 'conditional censure'.[4] Although this action had no basis in the treaties, it indicated Parliament's desire to keep the Commission accountable, while at the same time demonstrating its own institutional maturity: had the Parliament gone so far as to dismiss the Commission it would have been accused of over-reacting, not least because the incumbent Commission could scarcely have been responsible for the crisis.

The European Parliament also has the job of scrutinizing the Commission's management of the Community budget. Working with the Court of Auditors, the EP endeavours to ensure that European funds are adequately accounted for. Once the Parliament is satisfied that the budget for a particular year (usually two years later) has been adequately accounted for, together with the Council (Article 276 TEC), the Council making the recommendation, it grants the Commission

---

4.   For full details of the BSE crisis and the institutional responses see Westlake (1997).

'discharge'. In March 1998 the EP postponed granting the Commission discharge for the 1996 budget. By December 1998, the EP's Budgetary Control Committee had recommended accepting the Commission's accounts, but the December plenary session decided to refer the matter back to the Committee as a result of allegations of fraud and 'irregularities' (European Parliament 1998e). The Commission President threw down the gauntlet, suggesting that if the Parliament would not discharge the 1996 Budget they should formally censure the Commission.

Technically the vote on discharge did not necessitate a censure, although logically if MEPs felt that the Commission was not competent in its financial affairs, there was scope to claim it was generally incompetent and should go.[5] On 17 December, the leader of the Socialist Group, Pauline Green, plus 70 Socialist colleagues tabled a censure motion, which was intended to demonstrate the Parliament's confidence in the Commission rather than to sack it. However, in the following weeks, claims of fraud, cronyism and other forms of maladministration received much publicity. The position of the European Commission looked very weak by the time of the votes in the EP's plenary session on 14 January 1999. Some centre-right MEPs were keen to censure individual Commissioners, and indeed forced votes of confidence on Commissioners Edith Cresson and Manuel Marin. Both survived and the overall vote of censure was also defeated. However, the margin of support for the Commission was considerably less than in previous censure votes (see Westlake 1994b: 28)—out of 552 votes, 232 were in favour of censuring the Commission, 293 were opposed, while 27 MEPs formally abstained. Moreover, the Commission's survival was linked to an agreement to establish an independent committee to tackle fraud—there was no assumption that the Commission had simply escaped with allegations of financial irregularities still circulating. Arguably, MEPs had flexed their muscles effectively. The Parliament was able to secure compromises from the Commission without having to resort to the 'nuclear device' of the censure procedure outlined in Article 158, which might have back-fired if the EP had been seen to have acted irresponsibly. The implications of the Commission resigning are potentially profound and could have rendered EU business virtually impossible.[6] If this had occurred, the Parliament's reputation could

5. For a discussion of the right of discharge and the question of censure, see Westlake (1994b: 28-30).
6. In fact, following the resignation in March 1999, the outgoing Commis-

have been diminished rather than enhanced. By pulling back from censure and securing the Committee of Independent Experts, the EP managed to force the Commissioners to accept responsibility for its mismanagement and resign before they were pushed.

The right of censure is more important to the Parliament than actually using that power; it enables the EP to exert influence over the Commission, whereas actually sacking the Commission could lead to a diminution of the EP's public standing.[7] The EP also shares budgetary powers with the Council. However, as with the vote of censure, although the Parliament has the right to reject the budget, MEPs must use this 'nuclear weapon' judiciously to avoid accusations that they are irresponsible.

Financial Powers
Whereas Bagehot argued that budgetary powers were insignificant, in the late twentieth century they are of considerable importance and national elections frequent hinge on budgetary issues. The treaties establishing the EC gave the Parliament a very minor part in the budgetary process. However, the need for parliamentary accountability following the introduction of Community 'own resources' in 1970 altered the situation considerably. It was recognized that national parliaments would no longer be able effectively to scrutinize resources going to the Community budget. Hence the EP was granted countervailing powers via the 1970 Treaty amending Certain Budgetary Provisions of the Treaties and the 1975 Treaty amending Certain Financial Provisions of the Treaties. Although the changes did not enable the EP to *raise* revenue, they did give it a clear *financial* function. MEPs only began to make serious use of the budgetary powers after the first direct elections, rejecting the draft Community budgets for 1980 and 1985 and the 1982 supplementary budget. Parliament may vote 'by a majority of its component Members and two-thirds of the votes cast' to reject the draft budget, whereupon it is returned to the Council (European Parliament 1998a: Annex IV, Article 6.2). The problem with rejecting

sioners continued to act in a temporary capacity and after the initial confusion and controversy within the College, it was almost 'business as usual'.

7.   Parliament was in a difficult position in January 1999: the German press condemned it for not sacking the Commission, the French saw the episode as bad news for the Commission. This section and the next draw on information from Michael Shackleton.

the draft budget is that the EP is then unable to increase spending on its own preferred projects, since the default mechanism ensures that the amount of funds available until the question is settled is only one-twelfth of the annual budget for the previous year. In practice, therefore, the EP's ability to alter specific budget lines gives it greater influence in the budgetary process. While this affords the EP certain powers not enjoyed by most national parliaments, their use receives little attention from the media.

While the Commission proposes the budget, the Council and the Parliament are the twin budgetary arms of the Union. Both must agree the overall budget, but within that the Council has the final say on 'compulsory' spending, which arises 'necessarily' from the Treaties; the EP has the final say on non-compulsory spending. Over the years the balance has shifted from compulsory expenditure, which used to represent over two-thirds of the budget (most of it going to finance the Common Agricultural Policy) towards non-compulsory expenditure, as the Union has taken on new commitments. Thus the EP's budgetary powers have risen accordingly. Moreover, MEPs have challenged the Council on what counts as compulsory expenditure, thereby increasing their own powers further (Smith 1995a: 78; European Parliament 1994f). In 1997 the Parliament secured an Inter-Institutional Agreement (IIA) with the Council to the effect that spending on the Union's Common Foreign and Security Policy should be considered as non-compulsory expenditure, hence giving the Parliament a voice in this area of essentially intergovernmental policy-making, although at the price of losing the right to put such monies into reserve, which it had previously found useful (Spence 1998).

Over the years the practice of negotiating annual budgets has been modified by the introduction of inter-institutional agreements which give guidelines ('financial perspectives') for a multi-annual period (European Parliament 1994f: 8). The first such agreement was negotiated in 1988, with a second in 1993. An IIA offering a degree of flexibility for the period 2000–06 was agreed in December 1998, but a new IIA for a third financial perspective was not due until after the Agenda 2000 negotiations were completed. This practice altered the Council/Parliament balance: in December 1998 the Parliament secured the right to be involved in transferring amounts for both compulsory and non-compulsory expenditure, viewed as a step towards 'real co-decision on the EU budget' (European Parliament 1998b: 2). The EP's role in budgetary affairs is highly significant, since it has a much larger say than most national parliaments, which can rarely increase expenditure even within the tight restraints under which the EP operates.

Legislative Powers
In the legislative sphere, the Treaties of Rome granted the Commission sole right of initiative and the Council of Ministers the sole right to accept or reject the proposal; the Parliament's role was confined to the right of consultation (Article 7 of the EEC Treaty), although even this limited power represented an increase compared with the Treaty of Paris. Moreover the Council was not required to take the EP's views into consideration and at first would even pass legislation which differed significantly from the Commission proposals on which the EP had given opinions. Ironically in light of the failure to create a common electoral system for European elections, the Parliament's sole right of legislative initiative was to make proposals for a uniform electoral system—Article 138, para. 3 EEC Treaty; Article 108, para. 3 Euratom Treaty (Article 191 TEC).

1. *Consultation procedure*. The consultation procedure was extended under the Treaty on European Union to cover the newly created common foreign and security policy, and justice and home affairs pillars, on which the Parliament holds an annual debate (respectively Articles J.7 and K.6 TEU; new Articles 17 and 34 TEU). The Court of Justice's 1980 *Isoglucose* judgment (ECJ Cases 137/79 and 138/79) helped the EP to increase its influence in legislative process. In this ruling the Court declared an act void, arguing that the Council had contravened Article 173 by failing to receive the opinion of the EP before taking its own decision. This interpretation of the Treaty led the EP to change its Rules of Procedure in order to maximize its influence by delaying its opinions on Commission proposals if it is not satisfied with the response to its amendments. Similarly, the EP has adopted a procedure for 'renewed consultation' in cases where the Commission proposal has been altered dramatically from the version on which the EP has given its opinion, in order to prevent the Council ignoring the EP's opinion.

2. *Cooperation procedure*. The Single European Act established a cooperation procedure which increased the EP's role in the legislative process, particularly on issues relating to the '1992' internal market

programme. Whereas under the consultation procedure the Council is free to ignore the views of the Parliament, under the provisions outlined in Article 149 of the EEC Treaty as amended by the Single European Act, the cooperation procedure gave the EP a right of amendment, and enhanced the Parliament's relative position in the legislative process. If the Commission accepts the EP's proposed amendments, then the Council can only reject the amended proposal by unanimity, whereas it only needs a qualified majority to accept it.[8] Article 189c of the Maastricht Treaty extended the existing cooperation procedure to most areas of legislation where the Council takes decisions by qualified majority voting, with the marked exceptions of agricultural policy and external commerce. However, with the exception of some areas of economic and monetary union, where cooperation is in force and which the Treaty of Amsterdam left virtually unchanged, the procedure will virtually disappear under the provisions of the Treaty of Amsterdam, which seeks rather to extend the use of the co-decision procedure (Duff 1997: 142).

3. *Co-decision procedure*. Article 189b of the TEU (Article 251 TEC) established the co-decision or 'negative assent' procedure, which gives MEPs the power of veto in several policy areas. Only fifteen Treaty items were initially covered by the procedure, but they encompassed broad areas including the majority of internal market legislation, public health, consumer protection, and educational and cultural measures. Assuming that none of the institutions wants proposals to fall, it is necessary to secure agreement before the Parliament exercises its ulti-mate sanction of veto. Article 189b makes provision for a Conciliation Committee in which the Council and Parliament attempt to reach such agreement. A member of the Commission, almost invariably the Commissioner responsible for the particular issue, will attend the Conciliation Committee. While this situation might appear to give the Commission added leverage compared with the treaty provisions, which do not allow it a role in the conciliation procedure, in reality it merely serves to show the weakness of the Commission at that late stage in the legislative proceedings: it can no longer withdraw its proposals and cannot prevent the Council and Parliament reaching an agreement it does not like. The Treaty of Amsterdam extends co-

8.   For a further analysis of the cooperation procedure see for example, Bogdanor 1989a; Fitzmaurice 1988; Ollerenshaw 1993.

decision to a range of new treaty competences and also streamlines the procedure, which in its TEU formulation was extremely complicated. The experience of co-decision and the Conciliation Committee has been positive: four years after the introduction of the procedure it did not seem to have made the decision-making process any slower and had certainly increased the Parliament's influence. Yet the nature of co-decision, its complexity and lack of transparency raised certain problems: it might be easy to explain to voters that a parliamentary majority is necessary to get through legislation one wants, but the fact that conciliation occurs behind closed doors makes it difficult to demonstrate parliamentary powers to the average European voter.[9]

4. *Assent procedure*. Articles 8 and 9 of the Single European Act require the EP to give its assent, *inter alia*, to accession and association agreements. This power gives the Parliament a huge amount of leverage, since it can block major changes to the Union. The large number of applications for membership in the mid-1990s seemed to offer the European Parliament an important new bargaining tool. In 1992 some MEPs threatened to reject the applications of Austria, Finland, Norway and Sweden if further institutional reforms were not undertaken in addition to those in the Maastricht Treaty. No such reforms came about, yet in May 1994, the EP gave overwhelming support to the accession agreements. MEPs appeared to have missed a great opportunity to show voters their importance. In reality, the EP suffers from the same problem here as in its powers to dismiss the Commission: the power is a 'nuclear' one, which parliamentarians are reluctant to use, both because it might result in criticism of them for being irresponsible and because, in the case of enlargement, rejection would have entailed rejecting something MEPs themselves supported.[10]

The EP wields a considerable array of powers, although by 1999 it still did not have the right of legislative initiative, which remained the domain of the Commission (and, in the second and third pillars, of the Council). Nevertheless, MEPs were able to influence Community (as

9.　For a fascinating and detailed outline of the co-decision procedure and its impact on EU decision-making, see Maurer 1998.

10.　Given the party fragmentation within the European Parliament (discussed in the following chapter) and absenteeism, it has traditionally been rather difficult to secure an absolute majority, although the practice of co-decision, which has similar voting requirements, has led to greater discipline among MEPs.

opposed to Union) legislation significantly and MEPs had recognized the Commission's sole right of initiative as an important part of the overall institutional balance, with MEPs concentrating on maximizing their treaty-based powers to achieve maximum influence within the Union.

The Role of the EU as a Political Subsystem

The argument that there is 'less at stake' in European elections rests on two assumptions: first, that the European Union represents a less important political arena than the Member States; secondly, that the European Parliament wields fewer powers within the political system than its national counterparts. As already shown, while it is easy simply to claim that the EP plays only a small part in the decision-making and executive-forming processes of the EU, this ignores the pertinent question of the powers and functions enjoyed by other (national) parliaments/legislatures. The rise of political parties and of the mass media has reduced the role of national legislatures in the twentieth century, so that, by comparison, the EP is not a weak institution.

The increase in legislative business arising at the European level means that the European Union had a much greater influence on the daily lives of citizens and on the legislative agendas of the national parliaments in the Member States in the 1990s than in 1979.[11] Issues ranging from unemployment and immigration to the apparently trivial matter of bananas were all subject to decisions at the European level (Stevens 1996). The characterization of the European Union as still a subordinate political system had therefore become contentious, at least in terms of policies covered. The nature of the EU as a political system remained hybrid, however, with a certain ambiguity in the decision-making processes (Wallace 1996).

On Norton's redefinition, the European Parliament can be characterized only as a 'modest' parliament, since it lacks the right of initiative. Yet in this it differs little from most national legislatures in Western Europe: an analysis in 1990 of seven such institutions—the British House of Commons, the French *Assemblée Nationale*, the German *Bundestag*, the Italian Chamber of Deputies, the Irish *Dáil*, the Dutch *Tweede Kamer* and the Swedish *Riksdag*—showed all to be 'modest' as

---

11. Analyses of the increasing EU competences are given by Pollack (1994) and in several chapters of Wallace and Wallace (1996).

well (Norton 1990a), so that the European Parliament cannot be seen as less significant than many national parliaments. This finding would, on first inspection, suggest that the European Parliament should be viewed as at least the equal of its national counterparts.

In fact, the increase in the scope of decision-making at the European level, coupled with the changes to the formal powers of the Parliament, meant that by 1999 the EP was in many ways more powerful within its subsystem than the national parliaments. Many of them could affect European legislation in only a limited way, and their ability to enact legislation at the national level had also been severely constrained both for the reasons mentioned above and because of the growing scope of European legislation. Only the Danish Common Market Relations Committee had any real control over the ministers who were responsible for decisions taken at the European level, insisting that ministers act on a mandate from the Committee. Elsewhere national parliamentary scrutiny of European legislation was much weaker (see European Parliament 1998c). The European Parliament, by contrast, could both scrutinize European legislation and in some cases affect its outcome.

Norton (1990a: 5) claims that European parliaments have succumbed to the dominance of executive forces and that this is why they do not have strong legislative powers. This explanation is not appropriate in the context of the European Union, however, since the EP is not dominated by the executive (although the Commission does have the right of legislative initiative denied to the Parliament) but rather by the Council of Ministers, whose role is not well defined. Although the Council of Ministers is composed of members of *national* executives, in their guise as members of the Council of Ministers they perform a *de facto* legislative function.

However, there is a further function of parliaments to consider, namely 'regime support', the level of which does contribute to various characteristics of European elections such as low turnout and emphasis on domestic issues. As Norton (1990a: 4) puts it:

> Legislatures variously fulfil significant regime support functions. Study of these functions shifts the focus away from that of the relations of legislature to executive to that of legislature to the citizenry.

'Support', which he defines as 'a set of attitudes that look to the legislature as a valued and popular political institution', is also the second variable in Mezey's typology (1979: 156). It is this aspect of parliamentary functions that is lacking in the European Parliament. The fact that the election is not for a national institution is important, since national loyalties continue to predominate, despite the symbolic establishment of European citizenship via Article 8 of the TEU (Article 17 TEC).

As Norton (1990b: 147) points out, people's affective attachment to a national parliament frequently bears little relation to the powers that the parliament actually enjoys, depending rather on the political culture in the country. Feelings of identity are an essential part of the creation of a political community, which in turn is necessary for the functioning of a political system. Those feelings appear to be weak in the context of the European Union.[12] *De facto* powers alone are not enough to create the sense of attachment to the European Community/Union that neofunctionalist theorists believed would emerge as people gradually became aware of the benefits of the European enterprise. Without such a sense of community, it will be difficult to evoke significant interest in European elections. Thus, regardless of the substantive powers conferred on the European Parliament and the functions it performs, the relatively weak sense of European identity, coupled with public perceptions of a weak Parliament, mean that European elections are ill-placed to fulfil the expectations of their advocates, or the fears of those who were hostile to the idea of a directly elected European Parliament. Politicians and political parties could, of course, endeavour to foster such a community through their election campaigns.

Many of the EP's new powers require an absolute majority of MEPs—the Assent procedure, for example, requires an absolute majority of MEPs to support a proposal to allow an applicant state to join the EU, and the cooperation and co-decision procedures both require an absolute majority of MEPs to amend or reject Commission proposals. Initially it seemed that fragmentation within the EP and frequent absenteeism might stop MEPs making full use of their new powers. In practice, they exercised them very effectively in the 1994–99 Parliament.

In order to secure a majority in the EP, however, coalition-building is necessary. This frequently means that the two largest groups, those of the European People's Party and of the Party of European Socialists, vote together. Thus while treaty reform has increased the role of the European Parliament, it has also fostered a need for cross-party cooperation of a kind which makes it very difficult for parties to campaign on

---

12. See, for example, *Eurobarometer* data on attitudes towards national and European identity.

their achievements in the outgoing parliament. In theory the EP's increased role in decision-making should have rendered it easier for politicians, parties and journalists to interest voters in the elections; yet the difficulty of differentiating between the parties has, perhaps, been exacerbated, partly off-setting the gain. The exception could prove to be the vote on the Commission Presidency, which would give an opportunity for parties to stress the importance of securing a majority for the Left or Right and hence give something for voters to rally around. The resignation of the Santer Commission and its replacement in the late spring/summer of 1999 seemed to offer considerably more scope for the parties to campaign on this basis than had been the case in previous EP elections discussed in the following chapter.

5 |

Political Parties at the European Level

> Only direct elections can lead to the formation of political parties orga-
> nized at the European level, elected for their ability to cope with prob-
> lems at the only level where solutions may be found, responsible to
> electors from many different states (Beesley 1963: 82).

Political parties play a major role as interest mediators in most representative democracies. Their activity in the European Union has been
rather more ambiguous, however, with party politics essentially predicated on national political activity. European level political parties have
not developed in the way many protagonists of European elections
envisaged, leading many to assume that transnational parties did not
matter and were ineffectual. However, such an analysis does transnational parties a disservice: the tendency is to assess such bodies by the
standards of national political parties; since the EU is a *sui generis*
organization, perhaps transnational parties too should be evaluated by
different criteria. This chapter considers the nature of transnational
political parties, noting that while transnational party activity has been
limited in the electoral arena, development has been considerably
greater outside the electoral framework. Member States' politicians
meet colleagues from their sister parties from other Member States and
the Groups of the European Parliament prior to European Council
summits (Hix 1993). Similarly, cooperation between parties from different Member States is greater within the EP than that experienced at
the time of elections. Examination of the role the transnational parties
play in creating manifestos and campaigning will thus be supplemented
by an assessment of the activities of national political parties during the
elections.

At the electoral level, the inability of candidates to raise 'European'
issues such as asylum and immigration, EU enlargement and unemployment is the almost inevitable result of the absence of a European
party system beyond the relatively weak party federations and so-called

'transnational parties', based on the national systems of the various Member States. This in turn is partly the result of the multiplicity of electoral systems in force for European elections. The method of European decision-making, whereby the Council of Ministers tradition-ally has the final word on legislative matters, also means there is little incentive to campaign on specific policy matters in the European elec-tions. Finally, the absence of transnational media also impedes transna-tional campaigning. All of these factors have led to a situation where, by the time of the elections in 1994, although transnational cooperation had increased, the main focus of the elections was still national.

Parties at the European Level

Prior to the introduction of direct elections, Dutch Socialist MEP Henk Vredeling observed that:

> A curious phenomenon may be noted within the European Commu-nity...the *absence* of any moves towards European integration among the political parties in the member states (Vredeling 1971: 450).

Twenty years later, Article 138a of the TEU (Article 191 TEC) states:

> Political parties at European level are important as a factor for integra-tion within the Union. They contribute to forming a European awareness and to expressing the political will of the citizens of Europe.

This difference in tone might reflect an evolution of European political parties in the intervening period as many supporters of European elec-tions desired. The aim behind the insertion of political parties into the Treaty framework in 1991, at the suggestion of the Secretaries-General of the three main party families and of the President of the European People's Party (EPP), Wilfried Martens, seems to reflect a claim put forward by Michael Steed (1971: 169), to the effect that one of the less frequently cited arguments for such elections was 'as a means to the creation of trans-national political forces'.[1] Taking federal states such as the US as his model, Steed argued that political parties could play an important part in integrating the states of a federal democracy, '...the integrating party not merely combines state interests but by providing political loyalties which cut across state loyalties, it strengthens the federal loyalty' (Steed 1971: 468-69). Although he did not expect such

---

1.   For a detailed analysis of the emergence of Article 138a and an analysis of its possible implications, see Jansen (1998: 13-18).

powerful transnational parties to emerge at the European level, he thought that direct elections might contribute to their creation.

Cooperation between European political parties can be traced back to the party internationals, which date from 1947 in the case of the Christian Democrat grouping—the *Nouvelles Equipes Internationales* (from 1965 the European Union of Christian Democrats)—and the Liberal International, and from 1950 for the Socialist International.[2] Links were also swiftly established in the Common Assembly of the European Coal and Steel Community, where, for example, delegates from the various Socialist parties formed a Socialist Group in September 1952 and the Liberal parties a 'Liberals and Allies Group' on 20 June 1953 (ELDR 1995: 35). This development set the pattern for the subsequent workings of the European Parliament and led Leon Lindberg (1963: 89) to assert that 'cleavages were occurring on other than national lines, or that national interests were being subordinated to some notion of a Community interest'. While he noted that the members of these groups saw them as being precursors to 'European' political parties, he argued:

> if these parliamentary groupings are to develop into real European political parties, their activities will have to be coordinated with those of electoral parties organised on European and not national lines. This will only come with the introduction of direct popular elections for the Assembly (Lindberg 1963: 90).

Extra-parliamentary links remained more limited until the 1969 Hague Summit gave tentative support to direct elections, thus providing a stimulus for closer party cooperation (Pridham and Pridham 1979a: 64). The Confederation of the Socialist Parties of the European Community (CSP) was thus established in April 1974, shortly before the decision to hold elections was finally taken. The decision taken at the Paris Summit in 1974 to introduce direct elections by 1978 at the latest provided the main catalyst for the creation of transnational party federations.[3] European Liberal parties followed the Socialists in establishing the Federation of Liberal and Democratic Parties in the European Community (ELD) in March 1976. The stated aim of the ELD, which changed its name to the Federation of Liberal, Democratic

2.   For a full description of the early transnational party links, see, *inter alia*, Pridham and Pridham (1979 and 1981); Hix (1996); and Smith (1997).

3.   The first elections were postponed until May 1979 because of delays in Britain.

and Reform Parties (ELDR) in 1986, was 'the coordination of liberal policy leading up to the forthcoming direct elections to the European Parliament' (ELDR 1995: 7). The Christian Democrats established the European People's Party: Federation of Christian Democratic Parties of the European Community (EPP) in April 1976. The Green parties similarly formed a transnational grouping as they became established across Europe with the creation in June 1993 of the European Federation of Green Parties. All four of these parties/party federations extend membership or some form of associate membership to similar parties from the applicant states and sometimes even further afield.

The centre-right European People's Party, despite its subtitle of 'federation', declared itself to be a political party from the start. In November 1992 the Socialists followed suit, voting to call themselves the Party of European Socialists (PES), and in December 1993 members of the ELDR Council voted to become the European Liberal, Democrat and Reform Party. In the case of the PES the change was more than just semantic: votes on issues which are decided by qualified majority voting (QMV) in the Council of Ministers are now taken by majority vote in the PES.[4] The formal shift from federation to party did not have a major impact on the activities of the European political parties, at least in electoral terms. It was an important move symbolically, however, reflecting a belief that the introduction of Article 138a might offer scope for public financing of the parties, as opposed to such financing just being available for their groups in the European Parliament on which the parties are currently reliant for funds. Indeed, the transnational parties have begun to play an increasingly important coordinating role outside the Parliament, allowing cross-fertilization of ideas between national parties from the same party families. This has particularly been the case for the PES and EPP, whose member parties have tended to be in government. Thus, prior to meetings of Heads of State or Government and latterly prior to Council meetings, ministers have met with political allies from other countries at eve-of-summit meetings, which allow them to reach some degree of consensus prior to the main meetings (Welle 1998). This offers significant advantages to members of the largest transnational parties, the EPP and PES, since each national government is almost certain to contain at least one party of EPP or PES persuasion. Thus there has been a move towards European party political cooperation outside the electoral framework,

---

4.   Source: Interview with PES and PES Group officials in March 1994.

suggesting that Hallstein and others were wrong to assume that European elections were what was needed to create a European party system. Nevertheless, it should be borne in mind that such cooperation did begin in the context of the European Parliament, and it is in the parliamentary groups that transnational party activity is most obvious.

Party Groups in the European Parliament
Right from the start MEPs sat in transnational groups with other Members from like-minded parties. In the original Assembly, this was a reasonably simple set-up, with MEPs coming from three main party families—Christian Democrat, Social Democrat and Liberal. Since at that time the MEPs were appointed, the parliamentary balance was in line with that in national parliaments and, by extension, broadly in line with the balance in the Council.[5] The introduction of direct elections altered the situation considerably, rendering group formation considerably more complex and less coherent than had previously been the case.[6] Moreover, while the elections were designed to bring the people into the integration process, and it had been assumed that they would help foster European parties, in many ways the groups created since 1979 have had little to do with the election campaigns or their outcomes.

The three main groups in the European Parliament are based on the three transnational parties and membership of these groups is largely dependent on a national party's membership of the relevant European party (see Table 5.1).[7] By 1999, the PES and EPP groups housed MEPs from all the Member States. The ELDR, by contrast, had become a very northern based group, reflecting the limited electoral support for such parties in southern Europe and their increasing success in the north,

5. The situation within the EP was rendered even more simple since the Communists, who were strong in both France and Italy, were not permitted to sit in the EP until the 1970s.

6. This was in part a result of expanding the membership of the EP from 198 prior to 1979 to 410 when direct elections were introduced. The problem has been further exacerbated by repeated EU enlargements; following the accession of Austria, Finland and Sweden in 1995, the EP was expanded to 626 Members. The prospect of further enlargement, this time to the new democracies of Central and Eastern Europe, led to an agreement at the 1997 Amsterdam Summit that a ceiling of 700 should be set (Article 189 TEC).

7. The exceptions being *Forza Italia* and the British Conservatives who sit with the EPP Group but are not members of the EPP Party.

Table 5.1: Members of the European Parliament (as at 27 January 1999)

	B	DK	D	GR	E	F	Irl	I	L	NL	O	P	FIN	S	UK	Total
PES	6	4	40	10	21	16	1	19	2	7	6	10	4	7	61	214
EPP	7	3	47	9	29	13	4	36	2	9	7	9	4	5	17	201
ELDR	6	5	—	—	2	1	1	4	1	10	1	—	5	3	3	42
UFE	—	—	—	2	—	17	7	3	—	2	—	3	—	—	—	34
EUL/NGL	—	—	—	4	9	7	—	5	—	—	—	3	2	3	1	34
GREENS	2	—	12	—	—	—	2	3	—	1	1	—	1	4	1	27
ERA	1	—	—	—	3	12	—	2	1	—	—	—	—	—	2	21
I-EN	—	4	—	—	—	9	—	—	—	2	—	—	—	—	1	16
N-A	3	—	—	—	—	12	—	15	—	—	6	—	—	—	1	37
Total	25	16	99	25	64	87	15	87	6	31	21	25	16	22	87	626

Abbreviations:

B	Belgium	F	France	O	Austria
DK	Denmark	Irl	Ireland	P	Portugal
D	Germany	I	Italy	FIN	Finland
GR	Greece	L	Luxembourg	S	Sweden
E	Spain	NL	Netherlands	UK	United Kingdom

Source: European Parliament 1999c

especially in Denmark and the Netherlands.[8] The membership of these three groups has altered over the years not just as a result of differing electoral outcomes, but as the transnational parties have accepted new members. In some cases this has been the result of EU enlargement which has led to parties from new Member States joining transnational parties and their respective groups in the EP. In other cases the changes have arisen from a decision by a particular national party to change groups. Until 1992, the British Conservatives sat in the European Democratic Group (EDG), comprising themselves and two Danish MEPs. The decision by John Major's government to seek admittance to the EPP Group, which was granted after considerable deliberation, led to the disappearance of the EDG and, inevitably to an increase in the size of the EPP Group.

Expansion of party groups does not only mean a growth in numbers, however; it can lead to a considerable shift in the ideological basis of a group and/or party. Originally the EPP was the most cohesive of the European party coalitions in ideological terms, but its homogeneity gradually eroded with the entry of Greek, Spanish and French MEPs whose approaches to European integration are frequently at odds with those of the traditional Christian Democrat members. The French parties, for example, sit uncomfortably with the EPP. The Giscardians who were previously in the ELDR are more at home in the EPP, even though most would not see themselves as within the Christian Democratic tradition. British and Danish Conservative MEPs are not members of the EPP: they sit as 'allied members' of the EPP Group and are therefore not technically involved in the manifesto process. This arrangement enables the parties' MEPs to take a full part in the activities of the EPP Group—provided they 'subscribe to the basic policies of the Group of the European People's Party and if they accept the Rules of Procedure' (Article 5b of the Rules of Procedure of the Group of the European People's Party [Christian Democratic Group] in the

8.   The ELDR Group was considerably weakened in November 1996 by the loss of the Portuguese Social Democrats (PSD), who switched to the EPP Group following a decision by the national party to defect from the ELDR *Party* to the EPP Party. This change, which was seen as a way for the PSD to gain 'credibility by association' with the governing Christian Democrats in Spain and Germany, for example at the eve-of-summit meetings mentioned above, is indicative of the way party group formation can change as a result of party political considerations without any reference to the peoples of Europe.

European Parliament)—while not having to make a commitment to the whole programme of the EPP. Thus for the 1994 European elections the British Conservatives made no reference to the EPP manifesto. By contrast, under Rule 5a of the EPP's Rules of Procedure, the *Forza Italia* MEPs agreed to the EPP programme when they joined the EPP Group, even though they did not join the Party either.

The Socialists, on the other hand, evolved from a fairly loose confederation of parties to become the most coherent transnational party, partly facilitated by a shift in the direction of the integration process from one that focused on free-market issues to one with a social dimension, which rendered the Union more acceptable to some previously hostile socialists. Socialization may also have helped increase the support of left of centre parties for the integration process—when the EC was created the governing parties were all Christian Democrat; as social democrat politicians in, for example, Britain and Greece, have become increasingly involved in the integration process, they seem to have become more positively disposed to the process.

Member parties of the ELDR family reflect widely diverging political cultures and historical developments and this is reflected in a party and a group which have at times been rather incoherent: the German Free Democrats (FDP) and Dutch Liberals (VVD) espouse a more economic liberal approach; the British Liberal Democrats and the smaller Dutch party Democracy 66 (D'66), which is also a member of ELDR, are social liberals, with a more positive view of the state and welfare. British Liberals have non-conformist origins, marking them out from their continental colleagues in Catholic countries who come from anticlerical traditions. Despite these differences, the core of the ELDR Party/Group has remained reasonably solid over the years, with only the more peripheral parties choosing to move in and out of the Group. For electoral reasons, however, the German Free Democrats were not represented in either the 1984–89 or 1994–99 parliaments and the British Liberals won their first elected Members only in 1994.

In contrast to the three main party families and to the smaller, but coherent Green Group, there have been a large number of rather ephemeral groups in the European Parliament that have arisen in some cases as 'marriages of convenience' rather than emerging from any transnational political trends. Since there are institutionalized advantages to being a member of a party group in terms of Committee chairmanships, rapporteurships and other official parliamentary functions, speaking time in plenary sessions, and financial and secretarial assistance, parties and MEPs have an incentive to cooperate within the Parliament to make the most of such opportunities. The minimum size for a group is determined by the EP's Rules of Procedure and has been revised following each enlargement of the Parliament. There is a bias in favour of transnational groups, since fewer members are required to form a group if they come from more than one country. From 1 January 1995 the minimum size for a Group was 29 MEPs if they came from just one Member State, 23 if they came from two Member States, 18 if they came from three Member States and 14 if they came from four or more Member States (European Parliament 1998b, Rule 29).[9] Groups which form within the Parliament but lack extra-parliamentary identities such as the European Democratic Alliance (EDA) composed of French Gaullists and Irish *Fianna Fáil* MEPs, may persist from one Parliament to the next, but do not campaign on common manifestos. Since they are typically formed only after the elections, supporters of such parties are not given much opportunity to know which parties their MEPs will be working with.

The weakness of the European party system means that, with the partial exception of the four transnational parties and party federations, the groups in the Parliament are highly fluid as shown in Table 5.2. During the lifetime of the 1989–94 parliament, two groups disappeared and several others saw minor changes in membership. The transitory nature of the EP groupings is highlighted by the fact that three new party groups were created in July 1994, an old one re-emerged and three groups vanished.[10] The technical Group of the European Right, which brought together far right parties, collapsed following disagreement between possible member parties (Pinder 1994). Following the elections, the Italian former fascists, the *Alleanza Nazionale*, refused to

9.   Those MEPs who are not members of any other group sit as 'Non-attached Members' and are treated rather like a group for practical purposes, being allocated speaking time, rapporteurships and other benefits. However, since by definition such Members come from very small parties with few allies, there is little incentive to be 'non-attached'.

10.   This phenomenon continued with the amalgamation in July 1995 of the European Democratic Alliance and *Forza Europa* to form the Union for Europe (UFE), an alliance which replaced the ELDR Group as the third largest in the Parliament, but one which had no electoral roots: French Gaullists had no idea when they cast their votes in 1994 that their representatives would subsequently sit with MEPs from the new Italian party.

Table 5.2: Groups in the European Parliament

Group[a]	Incoming 1989	Outgoing 1994	Incoming 1994	1999
PES	180	197	198	214
EPP	121	162	157	201
ELDR	49	44	43	42
UFE[b]	—	—	—	34
EDA	20	20	26	—
Forza Europa	—	—	27	—
EDG[c]	34	—	—	—
Green Group	30	27	23	27
EUL/NGL[d]	28	—	28	34
Rainbow Group[e]	13	16	—	—
ERA	—	—	19	21
I-EN	—	—	19	16
Technical Group of the European Right	17	12	—	—
Left Unity	14	13	—	—
N-A	12	27	27	37
Total	518	518	567	626

a. Following enlargement of the European Parliament in June 1994 to take account of German unification and on 1 January 1995 with Eftan enlargement, Parliament revised its Rules of Procedure, increasing the minimum number of Members required to form a group.
b. The European Democratic Alliance merged with *Forza Europa* in 1995 to form the Union for Europe Group.
c. This group disappeared in April 1992, when British and Danish Conservative MEPs joined the Group of the EPP.
d. This group, initially known simply as the Confederal Group of the United European Left, disappeared in January 1993, when the Italian former Communists, the PDS, joined the PES. The group reformed, with different membership, after the 1994 elections and added 'Nordic Green Left' to its name after Eftan enlargement in 1995.
e. The Rainbow Group ceased to exist after the 1994 European elections, but many of its members regrouped within the new European Radical Alliance.

Source: compiled from European Parliament (1994b, 1994d, 1999c) sit with the French Front National (FN) MEPs. Being unable to find another group willing to accept them, the *Alleanza Nazionale* MEPs were forced to sit as non-attached Members. However, partly as a result of the failure of the German *Republikaner* to breach the 5 per cent national threshold, the FN did not have enough allies from other far-right parties to form a group without *Alleanza Nazionale* and hence its members were also forced to sit as non-attached. Also among non-attached MEPs was the Democratic Ulster Unionist, Ian Paisley.

Left Unity, which had been composed of far left parties, was replaced after the 1994 elections by the Confederal Group of the United European Left.[11] The Rainbow Group, which had members from several countries in the 1989–94 parliament, disappeared after the election. Several members of that group, including the Scottish Nationalist Winnie Ewing, joined the newly formed European Radical Alliance (ERA), of which the largest component party was the French *Energie Radicale*, which owed much of its strength to the personality of its leader, Bernard Tapie.[12]

Forza Italia, at that time the main governing party in Italy, created its own group, *Forza Europa*, uniquely comprising only members of one national party.[13] Finally, a new group opposed to closer European integration, Europe of the Nations, was established. The bulk of its members came from the French anti-Maastricht list, *L'Autre Europe*, supplemented by two Dutch Protestant and four Danish representatives elected on the anti-integration lists—the People's Movement Against the Common Market and the June Movement. Although in the past there had been sections of the EP, notably several Communist parties and the British Labour Party, which were hostile to European integration, the

11. The Confederal Group of the United European Left had itself folded in January 1993 when the former Italian Communists, the Party of the Democratic Left (PDS), joined the Socialist Group.

12. *Energie Radicale* emerged from the much older, but less successful *Mouvement des radicaux de gauche*. The group was not led by M. Tapie but by former Secretary-General of the Council of Europe, Catherine Lalumière.

13. Following the accession of Austria, Finland and Sweden in January 1995, the Rules of Procedure were altered to increase the minimum size for a group. The national homogeneity was retained, however, because the two new Members came from the Italian Social Democratic Party and the Northern League. In July 1995 this grouping merged with the European Democratic Alliance to form the Union for Europe (UFE). However, in 1998 most of the *Forza* MEPs joined the EPP.

Europe of the Nations was the first parliamentary group whose organizing principle was opposition to further integration.[14]

The three newly formed groups in 1994, *Forza Europa*, the Europe of the Nations and the European Radical Alliance, were unusual in all being dominated by a single national party (to a greater extent than even the European Democratic Alliance). The only previous example of such national dominance was the European Democratic Group which comprised 60 British Conservatives and just two Danes in the 1979–84 parliament. *Forza Europa* had no *raison d'être* other than being the European parliamentary group of a new national party and its European policies were not clear when the group was formed. There was some speculation that the 27 *Forza* MEPs would join the EPP after the German general election of 1994, but at that stage this came to naught. Even when enlargement in January 1995 meant that *Forza* did not have enough MEPs to form a group by itself, the new recruits to the group were also Italian, thus temporarily ensuring that the *national* identity of the group remained. The subsequent alliance with the EDA may have reflected a *Europe des patries* approach to European integration, but more probably reflected a desire on the part of both groups to increase their influence in the EP. The defection of most *Forza* MEPs to the EPP Group was a triumph for the EPP, which had been actively seeking to expand its membership in a clear battle with the PES.

Campaign Activities

The main electoral functions of the European parties and party federations have been to formulate transnational manifestos and coordinate common campaigns. They have tended to leave the actual organization of the campaigns to national parties, something which has contributed to criticism of the parties as being little more than weak federations. Yet, as Klaus Welle (1998), the Secretary-General of the European People's Party, points out, national parties have the capacity to run election campaigns and it might therefore not be a good use of resources for transnational parties to attempt to replicate similar functions. One should beware of assuming that European level parties either should or will inevitably look like national parties as they have developed in Western Europe. For Welle, the principle of subsidiarity is not

14. The European Democratic Alliance was also hesitant about European integration, but its approach was more nuanced.

only important for EU decision-making, but also for parties at the European level. The absence of a common electoral system for European elections also helps foster a sense that European elections are a series of separate national contests.

Transnational parties do, however, play a large part in producing election manifestos, which are the product of negotiations between all the constituent national parties. Differing political traditions in Member States coupled with the fact that most national parties are themselves coalitions of different groups and opinions and the consequent need for compromise, plus the use of several languages in negotiating the manifestos mean that the documents which emerge are bland, offering little more than platitudes. Since the European Parliament does not set the legislative agenda of the Union, the manifestos have tended to be more symbolic statements of belief than statements of intent. Yet to expect them to be any more than this might be to set too high a standard: manifestos in national elections are used more as a way of articulating broad ideas and motivating party activists than to set out clear policy strategies. National parties have accepted the manifestos of the transnational parties they belonged to with varying degrees of enthusiasm and few make much use of the transnational manifestos in their campaigns. Even the most dedicated pro-European MEPs express reluctance to stress such documents, recognizing that a domestic focus will be more productive in securing votes.

Issues

The 1960 Dehousse Report (para. 23) argued that European elections should be held on the same day in all six Member States, but that they should not coincide with national elections, general or local, in any of the Member States, since:

> there would be a real risk that the distinctive character of European elections would be overshadowed by local or national issues brought forward by parties or candidates during the electoral campaign. This would undoubtedly imperil one of the principal aims of European elections—to increase the peoples' interest in European unification.

However, by the time direct elections were finally introduced in 1979, it was decided that the benefits in terms of higher turnout which might accrue were such that simultaneous national and European elections should be permitted (Patijn Report 1974: 26). National issues *have* dominated when national and European elections have coincided;

turnout has indeed been considerably higher when national and European elections have been held on the same day. In fact, despite the creation of transnational party federations and regardless of whether they coincided with national elections, direct elections in each Member State have been dominated by national parties fighting on domestic issues, admittedly often intermingled with European issues.[15]

In 1994 there were many EU issues which could have served as a basis for election campaigns, but the political parties seemed reluctant to act on them. By the 1994 elections, many questions concerning European security, internal and external, had emerged for the first time in 40 years, following the collapse of Communism and German unification. In addition the long-term recession in Europe meant governments were facing record high levels of unemployment. Some of these issues could have served as the basis of transnational European campaigns. The most important of them were the high levels of unemployment across the EU, the prospect of a common currency, immigration, the failure to act effectively in former Yugoslavia, EU enlargement to include the Eftan states—Austria, Finland, Norway and Sweden—and environmental issues (Smith 1994: 32-33).

Environmental issues are particularly interesting: many transcend national borders; environmentalist or 'Green' parties have been successful in several West European countries; and under the Maastricht Treaty (TEU) the EU, and especially the EP, has a considerable degree of influence in environmental policy.[16] Thus by 1994 there was one policy area in which the EP had a clear role in the decision-making process and which did not cause internal divisions within national parties—few politicians in the 1990s would deny the importance of the environment—that could have served as a basis for a campaign on European issues.

However, although all the issues mentioned above were of concern to European elites at the time of the elections, they did not all feature prominently in election manifestos. Even when an issue featured in the transnational manifestos, whether it was actually raised during the

15. For a full assessment of the campaigns in the 1979, 1984 and 1989 elections see Herman and Lodge (1982); Lodge (1986) and Lodge (1990).

16. Under the terms of the Maastricht Treaty, the co-decision procedure was applied to large amounts of environmental policy and many of the co-decision procedures and conciliations taking place between 1993 and 1999 involved the EP's Environment Committee.

campaign depended on a set of factors, including the attitudes of national political parties and media preferences.

Transnational Manifestos
The transnational parties, including the Greens in 1994, produced manifestos, which their constituent parties could use as their main campaign literature or as a supplement to national manifestos. The PES noted in the preface to its 1994 manifesto that it was 'not a detailed programme, but rather a framework in which our future policies will be fleshed out'. A similar statement could be made about the EPP and ELDR manifestos. While this situation is the natural outcome of compromises between parties from several different states, it does precious little to arouse public interest in the elections. Only the Green parties, fighting for the first time on a transnational manifesto, put forward a rather different approach to European integration, focusing on ecological as opposed to economic growth and fair trade rather than free trade.

The EPP, PES and ELDR manifestos of 1994 differed from each other in detail rather than major substance; the Green manifesto was significantly different in terms of its vision of Europe.[17] Indeed by listing some of the key points of the manifestos without stating which proposals came from which parties, Galen Irwin (1995: 192-93) demonstrated how similar their policies were. The manifestos all mentioned the main policy issues at stake—unemployment; environmental policy; institutional reform, especially in terms of a reduction of the so-called 'democratic deficit' in European decision-making; economic and monetary union; a common foreign and security policy; asylum and immigration policy; and enlargement of the Union. 'European' issues were, thus, raised at least in the context of the transnational manifestos. Yet the manifestos did not give voters any clear choice about the future direction of the EU, either in terms of

---

17. In contrast to the first three elections, when the British and Danish Labour parties opted out of large sections the CSP manifesto (or 'Appeal to the Electorate' in 1979), the 1994 document contained only one footnote, to the effect that the manifesto must be read in the light of the Edinburgh Conclusions, which clarified the Danish position on the TEU. A similar proposal was debated and rejected by the ELDR Party, most of whose member parties felt that it would imply tacit support for more opt-outs in the future. This led the left-wing Danish Liberals, *Det Radikale Venstre*, to vote against the entire manifesto. For further details on the manifestos, see Smith (1994).

institutional change or policy options. The parties asserted their support for further integration, with commitments to more powers for the European Parliament and a written constitution, but did little to arouse public awareness of 'Europe'.

None of the manifestos made substantive proposals for a five-year legislative programme, which was quite natural given that the EP does not have a right of legislative initiative. The manifestos did not even touch on the Community budget either, a rather more significant omission, since MEPs do have a real influence over the budget. They all mentioned the main issues being dealt with by national and European elites at the time, but offered little in the way of hard policy proposals. This was especially true of the four-page EPP manifesto, perhaps least so for the PES manifesto, which offered some clues as to how a Europe governed according to its principles might try to tackle, for example, unemployment. Manifestos are typically compromises between different wings of a political party, and are designed to be presentations to encourage activists rather than to outline proposals. This is reinforced at the European level by the need to secure agreement between several parties and the fact that the EP has little power in several of those policy areas, such as internal security and foreign policy, which are of greatest interest to voters.

Little attention was paid in the 1994 manifestos to institutional reform or the need to increase the powers of the European Parliament, in marked contrast to previous manifestos. In the case of the PES this was partly the result of pressure from the British Labour Party which argued that institutional reform was not a vote winner and it was therefore better to concentrate on unemployment and the environment.[18] This seems to be a valid argument: domestic elections certainly tend not to focus on the minutiae of constitutional reform, nor on the detailed workings of legislatures; what matters is the impact the legislatures have on voters' lives. The parties recognized the futility of putting forward a clear five-year programme which there was no guarantee that the Commission would take up. However, this increased the difficulty of convincing voters of the relevance of European elections, either for themselves in their daily lives or for the future of the European Union, and thus gave little scope for the parties to mobilize public opinion across the Union. By 1994 the role of the transnational parties remained

---

18.   Source: comments from national and European Labour Party activists.

limited and although domestic and European politics were becoming ever more intertwined, national affairs still dominated.

Campaigns and Issues: The National Dimension

How much emphasis was placed on European issues and manifestos in the four sets of European elections varied from state to state and from party to party, depending on the point in the national electoral cycle and on national party attitudes to both European and domestic affairs.[19] Thus, where parties were internally divided, they were less likely to fight on European issues; where they felt that they were more vulnerable on domestic issues, they typically fought on European issues. Here the British Conservative Party offers a partial counter-example in 1994: bitterly internally divided over the future of European integration, the party chose to fight a campaign based on European issues. One explanation for this is that party strategists felt the governing party was even weaker on domestic issues. In 1994, the Spanish Socialist Party campaigned solely on the European manifesto in the hope of deflecting attention from domestic problems. Elsewhere parties were more reluctant to use the transnational manifestos. For example, although the British Labour Party did use the PES manifesto as its main campaigning document, it focused its campaign more on domestic policies, such as education.

In Luxembourg, where national and European elections coincided, the creation of European citizenship was a major election issue, because it heightened awareness among Luxembourgers of the numbers of non-nationals living and working in the country: 29 per cent of the electorate are non-Luxembourg EU nationals (Oliver 1996: 486). It is hard to categorize such an issue as European or domestic: rather it is an example of just how far domestic and European politics have become enmeshed.

In the Netherlands and Italy the European elections, occurring in the wake of general elections, took second place to continuing debates over the formation of governments. In Italy they were a test for the new *Forza Italia* movement of media magnate Silvio Berlusconi. The campaign suggested a shift away from the traditionally pro-integration stance of postwar Italian politicians, with the new foreign minister openly opposed to the TEU. The old regional list electoral system,

19. This section draws on material used in Smith (1996).

which had been replaced for the national elections in March, was used for the European elections, resulting in the main parties fighting separate campaigns, in contrast to the general election in which they fought in coalition. There was thus a possibility that the alliances forged for the general election might have broken down, which the parties were keen to avoid.

In The Netherlands, where the European elections came in the wake of a local election in March and a general election on 3 May and where the composition of the government was still not clear following the general election, the 1994 Dutch European elections were even more low-key than usual. Moreover, although the main political parties were all in favour of further European integration, media coverage was negative, with one commentator telling those who were hostile to European integration to abstain. Many of the issues raised in the campaign were European, especially immigration, drugs and the fight against criminality, but they are all issues which fell under the third pillar of the EU, over which the EP had little control.

With 19 elections—local, Federal and European—scheduled in 1994, Germany seemed even more likely than The Netherlands to suffer from voter fatigue. The European elections fell in the middle of the election period, ensuring the results would be used as an indicator for the Federal elections. The Christian Democrats (CDU), the Social Democrats (SPD) and the Free Democrats (FDP) all fought strongly pro-European campaigns despite the declining support for Europe among voters. These parties were opposed by a large number of anti-European or, more accurately, anti-Maastricht parties, the most prominent of which were the newly-formed *Bund Freier Bürger* led by the former member of Commissioner Bangemann's cabinet, Manfred Brunner, and the far right *Republikaner* which held eight seats in the outgoing European Parliament. Following German unification, the 5 per cent *national* threshold for representation meant that the CDU's sister party, the Christian Social Union (CSU), which only presents lists in Bavaria, needed to obtain around 40 per cent of the *Bavarian* vote to ensure it gained any European MPs. Prior to the elections Edmund Stoiber, Minister President of Bavaria and CSU leader, made some speeches rejecting a federal approach to Europe. This approach put him somewhat at odds with coalition partners, especially the extremely pro-European Chancellor Kohl. The CDU's campaign focused heavily on the personality and policies of the Chancellor. Similarly, the SPD emphasized its national leader, Rudolf Scharping, and the FDP the head of the European list and leading figures in the party such as Otto von Lambsdorff.

The British Conservative Party, riven over its policy towards the European Union, might have been expected to focus on domestic policies. However, because of very poor opinion poll ratings, they chose to concentrate on European issues, and in particular the defence of British sovereignty within the EU. By attacking the opposition parties who, they claimed, wanted to give up Britain's veto, the Conservatives hoped to woo back those voters hostile to further European integration. However, the deep divisions which campaign managers hoped had been quashed in the aftermath of the Maastricht ratification debate re-emerged. To an extent, the election campaign did open up discussion on approaches towards European integration, but it fell far short of giving voters a clear pro-system, anti-European or anti-Maastricht choice: splits *within* the Conservative Party proved to be deeper than those *between* the parties (*Financial Times*, 1 June 1994). The British electoral system ensured that such intra-party differences could not be translated into choices for the voters: in some constituencies voters were presented with an anti-EU Conservative candidate, in others a pro-EU person.

With the governing party divided on European issues the main opposition parties might have been expected to stress their more positive views. Yet, as Labour had done in 1989, they both used the election as a mid-term referendum on the Conservative government. In the words of the acting Labour Party leader, Margaret Beckett, the campaign would focus on the 'whole picture—Tory record in Britain and in Europe' (cited in Butler and Westlake 1995: 173). While Labour and the Liberal Democrats adopted the PES and ELDR transnational manifestos respectively, they concentrated more on national issues. The Liberal Democrats, aware that the Conservatives were likely to accuse them of being 'poodles of Brussels', were anxious not to emphasize their strongly pro-European attitudes. The election campaign was overshadowed by the death of the Labour leader, John Smith, and the subsequent speculation about his successor.

Like the British Conservatives, the ruling Socialist Party in Spain sought to minimize the effects of its domestic unpopularity by campaigning on European issues. Indeed, the pro-European rhetoric of Prime Minister González seemingly ignored the decline in popular support for European integration which had occurred since the previous EP elections.[20] The main opposition party, the Popular Party (PP) chose to emphasize domestic issues. This approach was taken because the PP, comprising Conservatives, Liberals and Christian Democrats, was internally divided over European issues: a campaign fought on European issues would only have revealed those divisions. Moreover, the PP hoped to benefit from the government's unpopularity and defeat the Socialists in a national poll for the first time. Corruption scandals in which certain prominent Socialists were implicated came to light during the election, ensuring that the focus of the elections was much more on national than European politics.

In France, parties of the moderate right were also divided on issues concerning European integration, with the Gaullist Rally for the Republic (RPR) typically cautious about closer cooperation with other states and the Giscardian Union for French Democracy (UDF) some-what more enthusiastic. Nevertheless, the two parties formed a joint list and pledged to fight on an EPP platform for the 1994 elections. The agreement represented a large shift for the RPR, but one it was prepared to pay to secure UDF support for its candidate in the 1995 presidential elections. Voters were thus deprived of a choice concerning approaches to European integration or over solutions to European problems.

However, European affairs featured prominently elsewhere in the French election campaign: anti-Maastricht campaigners Philippe de Villiers and Sir James Goldsmith created a 'Euro-sceptic' list, *L'Autre Europe*, which fought on an anti-integration platform. There was even a list concerned solely with the failure of European foreign policy in the war in Bosnia, *L'Europe commence à Sarajevo*, which called for the arming of Bosnian Muslims. Another new force which emerged was *Energie Radicale*, a pro-European left-wing list based on the old *Mouvement des Radicaux de Gauche*, which was led by the charismatic businessman Bernard Tapie. The creation of these lists sparked debate on European integration and European policy issues and, in the case of *Energie Radicale* and *L'Autre Europe*, gave voters an opportunity to vote for parties which did not correspond with those traditionally fighting national elections.

20. In spring 1989, 74 per cent of Spanish respondents told *Eurobarometer* that their country's membership of the EC was a 'good thing'; by spring 1994 this had fallen to 49 per cent (*Eurobarometer Trends 1974–90*; and *Eurobarometer 42*).

From the time of their first referendum on Europe—on accession in 1972—Danish voters had been offered a choice over issues of European integration. In 1994 as in previous European elections, the People's Movement against the EU, which had campaigned against Danish accession to the European Community in the 1972 referendum, presented an anti-integration list. In 1994 a more moderate offshoot of the People's Movement, the June Movement, created at the time of the 1992 TEU referendum, and opposing the EU but reluctantly accepting the reality of integration, also fielded a list. Thus Danish voters were given the opportunity to vote for candidates opposed to further European integration, even though all the main national political parties accepted the TEU subject to the Edinburgh Conclusions. Interest in the elections was enhanced by the candidature of several senior politicians, notably former Prime Minister Poul Schlüter. Schlüter campaigned for a Europe of nation states, and suggested that he would assemble a group of Danish MEPs in the EP, which would have represented a marked deviation from the pattern of transnational groups which had characterized the Parliament for the previous 40 years.

In Ireland, Greece, Portugal and Belgium campaigns were lack-lustre, evoking little public interest. In Greece this was partly due to the fact that the elections came only eight months after national elections. While there was discussion over Macedonia, there was no policy difference between the two main parties. Similarly, there was little to distinguish the parties in their approaches to the EU, in marked contrast to the first Greek elections to the EP when *Pasok's* approach was considerably more reluctant than that of New Democracy. However, *Pasok* and New Democracy did campaign on European themes, namely how best to further Greek interests within the EU.

The main parties in Portugal also campaigned on how to get a good deal from the EU, the Socialists arguing that the ruling Social Democrats were not maximizing their advantages. Reflecting declining Portuguese support for European integration these two pro-Maastricht parties avoided talking about a federal Europe. An element of choice on the future direction of the EU was provided by the Conservatives fighting on an anti-EU platform.

In Ireland the main controversies had little to do with European or national issues, but that two parties, *Fianna Fáil* and Labour, had imposed candidates in the Dublin constituency. There was little interest in the elections, despite widespread media coverage. The low-key campaigns in Belgium were characterized by a considerable amount of hostility to the EU caused primarily by the large numbers of franco-phone civil servants living and working in Brussels. This led the Greens to campaign against the large presence of EU institutions in the capital. The elections also saw the emergence in Wallonia of the National Front, a far right party. For the Liberal parties the main aim of the elections was to beat the Socialists, who were embroiled in corrup-tion scandals, and the Christian Democrats.

Analysis of the National Focus
By 1994, the scope of transnational campaigning remained limited: although the transnational parties offered some mechanisms for such activities, they were very much subordinate to activity at the national level in each of the Member States. The weakness of coordinated campaigning made it difficult to put forward clear platforms on which the transnational parties could act in the new Parliament. Yet 'European issues' could have featured more extensively in campaigns in the indi-vidual Member States. Why then did they play such a small part?

In their analysis of British electoral behaviour Butler and Stokes (1974: Chapters 13 and 14) assess factors which determine whether or not an issue is likely to prove important at an election. They consider that the feelings a voter attaches to a particular issue and his/her perception of the parties' positions on that issue are crucial in determin-ing the impact of the issues on the parties' fortunes. Issues, they claim, will have a significant impact on the elections if three conditions are fulfilled:

1. The issue should be salient for the public—some issues, such as immigration, tend to arouse strong attitudes among voters;
2. Attitudes towards the issue should be skewed, that is there should be a strong bias in favour of a particular policy choice, a condition which is most easily met when the choice is black and white;
3. The voters should perceive the parties to have distinct policy positions.

When all three conditions are met Butler and Stokes would expect the issue in question to have a significant impact on the result.

If we consider European elections in this framework, one possible reason for the marked reluctance to emphasize European issues emerges. Divisions on issues concerning European integration typically come *within* rather than *between* parties in the individual Member States. It is rare for the existing party systems to offer voters a clear choice on questions either of the direction or of the scope of future European integration. Parties of the extreme left or right may provide the only divergence from a general support for further European integration in countries such as Germany and The Netherlands where the main parties hold broadly similar views on questions of European integration. Parties are naturally reluctant to put much emphasis on European issues which will highlight differences, since they are anxious not to appear divided at the national level. This means that it is almost impossible for voters to associate clear European policies with particular parties. In 1994 this factor affected the two main parties in Britain and the parties of the moderate right in France, which were reluctant to reveal their internal differences on European affairs and hence presented platforms which hid as much as they revealed. In such a situation it was hard for European issues to have an impact on the elections.

The problem was compounded by the nature of the European party system, which has not emerged in the same way as the party systems of the individual Member States. In the introduction to their seminal work, Lipset and Rokkan assert that 'the party systems of the 1960s reflect, with few but significant exceptions, the cleavage structures of the 1920s' (1967: 50). Until the 1980s although social cleavages had shifted, the party systems which they had given rise to remained relatively stable.[21] The transnational parties, on the other hand, were created as federations of national parties and do not necessarily correspond to any cleavages at the European level. As Vernon Bogdanor (1990: 7) has suggested, 'The party system in the European Parliament is one that is mainly carried over from domestic party politics.'

In many ways, the European parties can best be seen as fora for national political parties to meet with other like-minded parties. The transnational parties and party federations reflect the lowest common

21. By the 1980s the situation had begun to alter: social cleavages had changed significantly as a result of an increase in tertiary employment and the decline of religious worship. While the party systems remained comparatively static there was an increase in post-materialist groups, such as the various ecology parties, which began to take support away from the established parties. See Dalton (1988: Chapters 7 and 8).

denominator of national political parties, rather than reflecting cleavages on European issues. Although there is some convergence between
the political parties from the various Member States, which has enabled
transnational parties (and, more importantly, party groups in the
European Parliament) at least to exist, these groupings are arguably not
relevant to problems at the European level (Bogdanor 1989b: 208-209).
Moreover, as noted in Chapter 4, the fact that on many issues MEPs
from the three main party groups vote together in the EP means that
there is little scope for the transnational groups to campaign on their
record in the outgoing parliament.

Even if European political parties were to offer distinctive policies, it
is not clear that Butler and Stokes's first condition would be met. While
some issues with a European dimension such as unemployment might
have a high degree of salience, those issues with the greatest salience
and which voters feel should be tackled jointly at the European level
are rarely those over which the EP has any influence. Immigration is an
issue of high salience in some of the Member States, notably France,
Italy, Germany and Luxembourg. In spring 1994, 54 per cent of
respondents felt that immigration should be tackled at the European
level, 40 per cent at the national level and 6 per cent did not know
(*Eurobarometer 41*). Yet immigration was not an issue on which
parties could hope to achieve much transnational cooperation: for the
French and the Italians, the problem is one of migration from or
through North Africa; for the Germans, of migrants from East and Central Europe; and for the Luxembourgers, the problem arises from the
high numbers of Portuguese migrant workers. The states, therefore, all
see different solutions to the problem. Moreover, even after ratification
of the Treaty of Amsterdam, the EP's powers in this area remain fairly
limited.

Nor are attitudes to the types of issue discussed above particularly
skewed. Unemployment typically arouses strong public reactions but
many issues of European integration do not spark such clearly defined
public responses. Thus, on a range of European topics, the conditions
for them to affect relative party strengths is missing, reducing the
parties' incentives to campaign on such issues.

In the poorest states of the Union—Greece, Spain, Ireland and
Portugal—government and opposition parties have been able to fight on
the question of which party would be able to secure the most money
from the European structural funds for their country, and who would

make best use of the funds. This sort of debate shows the interaction between domestic and European politics which is emerging as more policy areas are tackled, at least partially, at the European level. One might expect this sort of mingling to increase with further integration, giving a more European aspect to the elections. Yet although this would yield elections fought on European issues, it would also contribute to a continued national focus for the elections. Since the funds are finite, their distribution can be seen as a 'zero-sum game' in which the Member States are competing. This reduces the scope for transnational cooperation as parties are required to put national considerations above links with political allies, giving rise to a situation like that in the United States where candidates typically campaign on their ability to 'bring home the bacon'.

A major problem in organizing transnational campaigns and articulating European issues has been the absence of transnational media. Prior to the first European elections, Leo Tindemans (1976: 28) recommended that:

> a serious effort should be made to promote collaboration between *information* media, in particular radio and television, to encourage the spread of information and better knowledge of each other. Such collaboration will be of particular significance in the context of direct elections to the European Parliament which will provoke throughout Europe an electoral campaign on European themes.

His advice was not taken, however, and the media have paid little attention to the elections. National media continue to focus on national issues and national personalities, hence the increased interest in the 1994 Danish campaign where national figures were candidates. Similarly, national figures including future President of France, François Mitterrand, and future President of the Commission, Jacques Delors, stood in the first elections in 1979. This national focus reduces the incentive to campaign on transnational issues or to organize transnational campaigns. As one MEP noted after the first European elections, 'The election should have been fought largely through the media as are elections in constituencies of this size in the USA' (cited in Butler and Marquand 1981: 142).

Finally, some have argued that the absence of a common electoral system (an issue to be covered in the following chapter) makes it harder to conduct transnational election campaigns or to view the elections in anything other than national terms (Lodge and Herman 1980: 45; Duff

1994: 156). Moreover, the fact that, because of differing national cultures, elections did not take place on the same day in all the Member States has been seen by some commentators as a way of explaining the difficulties experienced in organizing common election campaigns (Lodge and Herman 1980: 60). The situation was particularly protracted in Denmark in 1994, with the ballot taking place on the Thursday, but the count being held over until the Monday in order to avoid the additional cost of counting votes on a Sunday. Such factors, coupled with the fact that the elections do not produce a transnational government, reduce both the practicality of fielding common lists and the incentive to do so.

If the Commission, the Commission President or some other executive body were to be appointed as a result of the elections there would be a greater incentive for activity in European elections (Bogdanor 1986: 175-76). The TEU marked a first step in this direction by altering the length of the Commission term to coincide with that of the Parliament at the same time as it gave the EP the right to vote on the appointment of the incoming Commission. The Treaty of Amsterdam goes a step further, offering MEPs a right of consultation on the nomination of the Commission President, which they could use to ensure that the Commission President comes from the same political family as the dominant force in the EP. This situation could have an impact in facilitating campaigning in the 1999 EP elections, since parties and candidates might be able to demonstrate the influence the election results would have on the Commission and potentially on the development of European integration.

Conclusions

Despite their titles, the Party of European Socialists, European People's Party and the Party of European Liberals, Democrats and Reformers are perhaps best seen as party federations. These European parties are not autonomous from the national member parties; only the EPP allows individual party membership, and the parties rely on funds from national parties and their groups in the European Parliament. Yet, as Thomas Jansen (1998: 8) points out, 'The individual members of the European parties are necessarily identical to those individual organisations at national, regional, and local level which support them', noting that in Germany it is only possible to become a member of the federal party by becoming a member of a local or district branch.

European parties, essentially visible to the electorate only during the election campaigns—and even then only to a very limited extent— seem to disintegrate into their constituent national parties between elections. This situation would not be unusual in the United States, where the names Republican and Democrat serve substantially to foster some sort of partisan identification at presidential elections. As Haas and Whiting (1956: 263) have pointed out:

> American political parties lack the ideological cohesion of specific inter-
> est groups. Instead, they are merely federations of regional, local, and
> frequently scattered political interests which find common advantage in
> formal cooperation in national politics.

However, the US pattern is so different from the Western European national model that the former gives cause for concern to many of those who favour democracy at the European level. There are two problems in particular: first, there is little scope for Europe's transnational parties actively to promote international integration. As weak, fragmented groupings bound together by similarities in *domestic* policy areas, the focus on *European* matters remains limited, not least because member parties differ in the scope and depth of their commitment to European integration. This contrasts with the situation in national integration, where:

> There is a great deal of evidence that 'mass parties' have fostered inte-
> gration, that they have created a new 'ethnic definition' with the nation
> representing the new community (Hayward 1971: 231).

Secondly, national party systems across Western Europe are breaking down. The old social cleavages on which they were based have weak-ened, leaving a less solid foundation for partisan identification, which is therefore gradually declining (Franklin and Mackie 1991: 245-46). Attempts to create European political parties around the established party 'families', which were based on cleavages that have broken down at the national level, reduce the likelihood of voters identifying with these supranational parties. Where attachments are weak at the national level, they are even more diffuse in the European arena. Deutsch asserts:

> The more varied and salient these mutually *cross-cutting divisions* are,
> the better for the acceptability of the emerging union. The history of
> such cross-cutting alignments of political parties, religions, and eco-
> nomic interests (all supplementary, modifying, and partly overriding the

old ties to the original units and regions) can be traced in the history of the unification of Britain, Switzerland, Italy, Germany, and the United States.

   ...in the successful cases of integration by political amalgamation, the main cross-regional political factions or parties stood for something new. They were identified with one or several *major cross-regional innovations* which were both important and attractive at that time and place (Deutsch (1968: 197).

European parties have not stood for something new and have done little to cut across national boundaries. Even within the EP, the willingness of politicians to cooperate across national lines has reflected a pragmatic desire to achieve certain results, rather than a shift towards new transnational cleavages. Indeed, several of the groups in the EP result from bargains made after the elections, giving voters little opportunity to vote for or against particular coalitions. This is in marked contrast to Lindberg's view that the fact that MEPs sat in transnational groups meant that 'national interests were being subordinated to some notion of a Community interest' (see p. 83 above). The situation suggests that by 1999 national influences continued to play a considerable part in the European Parliament as Gaullists such as Debré would have predicted.

6 |

The Electoral Dimension

> Inadequate mobilization of the public and a consequent poor voter turnout for the direct elections will entail the danger that the Parliament's influence and powers are not strengthened but weakened (Bangemann 1978: 331-32).

At the elite level, European elections up to 1999 seem to have supported Michel Debré's sceptical views about the possibility of transnational political realities. What then does the behaviour of the public show us? Turnout in the individual Member States was generally below levels in national elections, but there were few other discernible patterns in voter participation. Moreover, just as the campaigns were fought on a predominantly national basis, so the results could best be understood from a national perspective. Thus, the hopes and expectations of the proponents of direct elections did not appear to have been vindicated.

This chapter seeks to explain why voter participation was so much lower in the first four sets of EP elections than in national elections and why there were so many discrepancies between states right across the Union. It focuses on institutional factors such as compulsory voting which have been seen to affect turnout in other democracies and then considers other factors which might affect electoral behaviour in terms of turnout and/or results for the parties, for example attitudes towards the European Parliament and other aspects of European integration, referred to by Niedermayer (1990: 47) as 'Europeanness'. Such attitudinal factors may help explain the differences in turnout in European elections up to 1994, both between countries and between national and European elections within the individual Member States.[1] The focus

---

1.   The implicit assumption here is that 'pro-European' citizens in the various Member States are more likely to vote than are 'Euro-sceptics'. Although this assumption is not necessarily valid—in America low voter turnout is associated with high levels of regime support (Birch 1993: 80-81)—for reasons which will be explored below, such an assumption may be valid in the context of the European Parliament elections.

then turns to the results in terms of parties, looking in particular at whether there have been transnational trends in voting behaviour. In fact, in accordance with Reif and Schmitt's (1980) findings after the first European elections, I shall show that the main similarities between the Member States seem to be that the results are heavily dependent on the national political context, with large and governing parties typically performing badly.

Turnout in European Elections

The need for a high turnout has been stressed prior to each set of direct elections. This was especially so before the first set in 1979, when it seemed that a low turnout would undermine the legitimacy of the EP or at least prevent it from capitalizing on the opportunities that direct elections offered. While the EP was concerned that a low turnout might mean it was unable to increase its influence, the Commission was worried that it might be interpreted as an expression of no confidence in the EC; simultaneous national elections, it was felt, could potentially serve to avert this problem. Thus the Danish demand that simultaneous national and European elections be permitted seemed acceptable since as the Patijn Report of 1974 pointed out, there was, 'the advantage that—at least in the beginning—a higher turnout in the European elections could thus be achieved'.

Turnout in European Elections: The Differences
Turnout in the first four sets of European elections was low and declined slightly over time from 65.9 per cent in 1979 to 58.3 per cent in 1994.[2] The figures for individual Member States (see Table 6.1 and the Appendix) show that the apparent pattern masks significant differences between countries, both in levels and trends in participation and in how closely they reflect behaviour in national elections. Looking at the turnout figures for each country individually, it is possible to see which countries differed significantly from the European average and whether they followed uniform patterns of participation or not. Some countries (see Figures 6.1–6.4), notably Belgium, enjoyed high, trendless levels of turnout; others, especially Britain, have had low turnout

2.	Turnout in EP elections is low compared to that in most West European countries but not compared to that in some other states. For example average turnout in American presidential elections is below 60 per cent (Bowles 1993: 55).

with little trend; while yet others have had significant fluctuations, Ireland being a prime example: Belgium saw the least fluctuation over time, Portugal the most.[3]

Table 6.1: Turnout in European Parliament Elections: 1979–94

	1979 %	1981 %	1984 %	1987 %	1989 %	1994 %	mean %	st. dev %
Belgium	91.4	n/a	92.2	n/a	90.7	90.7	91.2	0.67
Denmark	47.8	n/a	52.4	n/a	46.2	52.5	49.7	3.21
Germany	65.7	n/a	56.8	n/a	62.3	60.1	61.2	3.74
Greece	n/a	78.6	77.2	n/a	79.9	71.2	76.7	3.84
France	60.7	n/a	56.7	n/a	48.7	52.7	54.7	5.16
Ireland	63.6	n/a	47.6	n/a	68.3	44.0	55.9	11.88
Italy	84.9	n/a	83.4	n/a	81.0	74.8	81.0	4.45
Luxembourg	88.9	n/a	88.8	n/a	87.4	86.6	87.9	1.12
Netherlands	57.8	n/a	50.6	n/a	47.2	35.6	47.8	9.26
Portugal	n/a	n/a	n/a	72.6	51.2	35.6	53.1	18.58
Spain	n/a	n/a	n/a	68.9	54.6	59.6	61.0	7.26
United Kingdom	32.3	n/a	32.6	n/a	36.2	36.4	34.4	2.23
Average turnout	65.9	78.6	63.8	70.8	62.8	58.3	63.2	18.40
Standard deviation	19.67	0	20.08	2.62	18.25	19.24		18.37

At first sight there are no clear transnational patterns in voter participation. In Belgium and Luxembourg turnout was very high, close to the levels seen in national elections. At the other extreme turnout in Britain and Denmark was around 40 per cent lower than the average for their respective national elections. Significantly, turnout in Denmark was also considerably lower than in the various referendums which have been held on EU issues.[4] The other countries have all had fairly low levels of turnout, with participation falling steeply in Portugal and The Netherlands. Britain is the only country where turnout rose in each of these elections, but since it started at 32.3 per cent in 1979 and was still only 36.4 per cent in 1994, this is not a particularly creditable achievement.

3.   The statistical analysis of the turnout in European elections is based on the author's doctoral thesis (Smith 1995c).

4.   Turnout in the five referendums, on entry to the EC, on the SEA, two on the Maastricht Treaty and one on the Treaty of Amsterdam, have seen turnout of 90.4 per cent in 1972, 75.4 per cent in 1986, 83.1 per cent in 1992, 86.5 per cent in 1993 and 74.8 per cent in 1998 respectively (Thune 1994: 317; Roberts-Thomson 1998).

Figure 6.1: Belgian Turnout

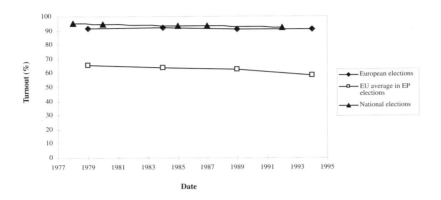

Figure 6.2: Irish Turnout

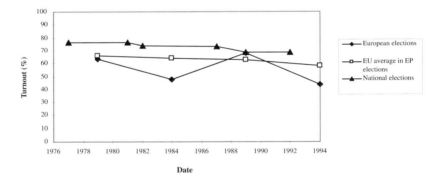

Determining Turnout

How then can we explain the phenomenon of low turnout in European elections? Research conducted into determinants of turnout in national elections has shown that several factors—institutional, socioeconomic and some related to the electoral rules in force—have an effect.

In his study of turnout in 30 democracies over a period of 20 years, G. Bingham Powell, Jr (1980: 26) found that 75 per cent of the variance in turnout in countries with competitive elections could be explained by compulsory voting, automatic registration (self-registration tends to result in lower turnout of potential voters), party competition and relationship between political parties and social cleavage groups. Others have found slightly different results, but similar patterns, with compulsory voting in particular a key factor. Powell (1980: 9-10) finds that making voting *compulsory* raises average turnout by approximately 10 per cent. The strength of sanctions makes a difference of course: *de jure* compulsory voting without the imposition of sanctions against non-voters may have little effect; conversely, *de facto* compulsory voting, such as has typically occurred in Italy, is likely to have a real effect.

Figure 6.3: Portuguese Turnout

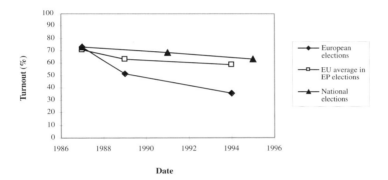

Figure 6.4: British Turnout

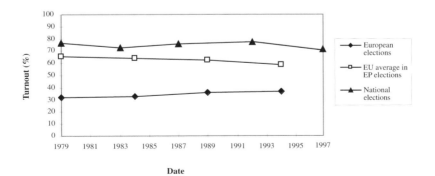

There is some evidence that the electoral rules in force also affect turnout. Almost all electoral systems yield results, that are to some extent disproportional (typically under-representing small parties) and both voters and parties are assumed to be aware of this. Parties react by fielding fewer candidates in areas where there is little chance of success; voters by switching from their preferred party to their 'more preferred' of the more widely supported parties to avoid 'wasting' their votes (Blais and Carty 1991: 80-81). This so-called 'psychological effect' also has an impact on turnout: while some voters would rather vote for a 'second-best' party in constituencies where their votes would otherwise be 'wasted', others may feel that there is little point in voting at all. Since plurality systems generally discriminate more against third parties than proportional systems do, one might expect turnout to be lower in plurality or majoritarian than proportional systems, especially where voters are aware of these distortions (Blais and Carty 1991: 89).

Turnout is also affected by whether or not electoral districts are *nationally competitive*, that is whether voters can have any real effect on the outcome of the election (Jackman 1987: 407). This factor affects the behaviour of both voters and parties. Powell (1986: 21) points out:

> Intuitively it would seem that in elections in which the outcome was expected to be close, citizens would feel more reason to participate and, perhaps more importantly, party organizations and activists would feel more incentive to get voters to the polls.

This hypothesis is supported in the US: 'Where a given election outcome seems a foregone conclusion, turnout will decline in that election' (Powell 1986: 19).

Nationally competitive constituencies are least likely to occur in single member plurality ('first-past-the-post') systems, such as Britain, where a Labour voter in Bournemouth or a Conservative voter in Sheffield has traditionally had almost no chance of affecting the result of a general election. In few cases will the result in one constituency have a decisive impact on the national outcome, and even within the constituencies individual voters will rarely have an effect on the result. As Blais and Carty (1990: 167) note, the problem is reduced with multi-member constituencies, which make it less likely that districts will be uncompetitive. A further, countervailing factor, not covered by this predominantly North American literature, is the role of voting as a symbol of group identity: this means that citizens will turn out to support 'their' candidate even in constituencies where the success of their preferred candidate is almost guaranteed. The problem at the European level is that voters may feel too distant from their representatives; that there is no-one who can be considered 'their candidate'. This is likely be particularly true when closed party list proportional representation (PR) is in force, since it offers voters no choice over the candidates.

Powell (1980: 18-19) finds that strong links between social groups and political parties exert a strong positive force on voter mobilization, stating that 'strong linkages between citizens' cleavage group membership and their party preferences are a powerful predictor of voting turnout across nations'. He asserts that this increased mobilization arises from two inter-related factors: with strong group ties, it becomes easier for parties to identify and mobilize their support; and for voters the voting decision is facilitated, they need only decide to vote, and the question for whom to vote does not really arise.

Party fragmentation and multipartism are generally (although not invariably) greater under proportional systems. Jackman (1987: 414), and Blais and Carty (1990: 178), find that *turnout declines as the number of effective parties contesting an election rises*. In the European context where parties tend to proliferate this might appear to be a significant factor in depressing voter mobilization. Coupled with the number of nationally competitive districts and the lower rates of disproportionality under proportional representation, the effect of PR on voter turnout would appear to be ambiguous. Controlling for exogenous factors, Blais and Carty find that turnout is, in fact, on average 5 per cent lower under majoritarian systems and 7 per cent lower with plurality systems than under PR, hence the electoral rules in force appear to have an effect on turnout.

Turnout: The Institutional Factors

Given that electoral rules clearly do have an impact on turnout, the fact that the Member States all have different electoral systems might help explain differences in turnout between the various states. Similarly, variations between the electoral systems used in national and European elections could explain differences within states, although in the main, electoral rules in the individual Member States have been fairly similar for national and European elections. This section considers institutional factors that have been found to affect voter mobilization and their possible relevance to European elections. Particular attention is paid to compulsory voting, simultaneity of national and European elections, and the nature of the electoral system. These features enable us to account for some of the difference in turnout levels *between* the Member States. The issue of party/social cleavage linkages which may help to explain differing levels of turnout *within* and *between* the Member States is then addressed.

How then might the varying electoral systems have affected turnout in the Member States? In the absence of agreement on a uniform electoral system, each Member State has determined its own rules of EP elections; the 1994 elections were held under 13 different electoral systems.[5] The accession of Austria, Finland and Sweden on 1 January 1995 led to the introduction of three more electoral systems, meaning that the 1999 elections would be fought with 16 different sets of electoral rules.

All bar one of the EU Member States have used some form of proportional representation in EP elections (see Table 6.2). Of those participating in the 1994 elections, eight had a single national constituency. To some extent the use of a single constituency is simply the result of each Member State having fewer seats in the EP than in the national parliaments; to keep constant the number of seats per constituency, and hence the degree of proportionality within each constituency, it is necessary to have fewer constituencies in EU than national elections.

Where there is a change to a single national constituency for European elections, as for example in Greece, proportionality may well increase, since the implicit threshold needed to secure election is reduced considerably. The main exception is The Netherlands, where the implicit threshold is actually higher in European than national elections, since both are fought in a single national constituency but there are 150 seats in the Dutch lower house, the *Tweede Kamer*, and only 31 Dutch seats in the EP. Elsewhere the lower threshold might be expected to lead to higher turnout, other things being equal, since votes are less likely to seem 'wasted'. However, the lower threshold could also contribute to party fragmentation or proliferation and this might act to reduce turnout. France, Germany, Greece and The Netherlands all have legal thresholds to prevent such proliferation. Additionally, there is the problem that larger constituency size reduces the links between representatives and voters—between MEPs and their constituents—and that may contribute to difficulties in mobilizing voters.

5.   The United Kingdom uses two systems: single transferable vote (STV) PR in Northern Ireland and the 'first-past-the-post' system in Great Britain.

Table 6.2: Electoral Rules in European Elections

Country	Number of seats	Number of constituencies	Electoral system	Choice of candidate?	Compulsory voting?	Restday voting?
Austria	21	1	Proportional: national list	Yes	No	Rest
Belgium	25	4	Proportional: regional lists	Yes, from party list	Yes	Rest
Denmark	16	1	Proportional: national list	Yes, from party list	No	Work
Finland	16	1	Proportional: national list	Yes	No	Rest
France	87	1	Proportional: national list	No, strict party list	No	Rest
Germany	99	1	Proportional: regional lists	No, strict party list	No	Rest
Greece	25	1	Proportional: national list	No, strict party list	Yes	Rest
Ireland	15	4	Proportional: single transferable vote	Yes, no list	No	Work
Italy	87	5	Proportional: regional lists	Yes, from party list	No	Rest
Luxembourg	6	1	Proportional: national list	Yes, open lists	Yes	Rest
Netherlands	31	1	Proportional: national list	Yes, from party list	No	Work
Portugal	25	1	Proportional: national list	No, strict party list	No	Rest
Spain	64	1	Proportional: national list	No, strict party list	No	Rest
Sweden	22	1	Proportional: national list	Yes	No	Rest
UK	87	85;12 from 1999	Plurality; from 1999, proportional: regional list; single transferable vote in Northern Ireland	Yes, no list; from 1999 no choice, strict party list	No	Work

Source: Compiled by the author from various sources including her own unpublished MPhil thesis, 'The European Parliament and Direct Elections' (1993); Mackie (1990); and Anastassopoulos (1998).

There is no fixed threshold for election under the single member plurality system used in Britain; a majority of one is sufficient for election. The implicit threshold can be very high and the larger constituency size in European elections compared to national elections further reduces proportionality. Moreover, the use of single member seats in Britain reinforces the distortionary effects of the plurality system. In some seats there will be little effective party competition. Everything being equal, this might be expected to result in turnout being lower in Great Britain than elsewhere.

Turnout in European elections has been 31.5 per cent higher in states which use some form of proportional representation. However, since Great Britain is the only country which has not used PR for European elections, the result is not statistically significant. One interesting fact is that turnout has been consistently higher in Northern Ireland, where a form of proportional representation is used, than in the rest of the United Kingdom. This offers some speculative evidence that turnout could be affected by the type of electoral system in force. However, it should be noted that turnout is also higher in general elections in Northern Ireland than in the rest of the UK and PR is not used then, which casts doubt on the significance of this factor. Here it seems that voter turnout might result from high levels of group identity which foster mobilization.

Voting is technically *compulsory* in Greece, Belgium and Luxembourg. Each of these three countries imposes a fine on non-voters. The penalty in Luxembourg for not voting is 1000–2500BFr for a first abstention, rising to 5000–10,000BFr for a re-offence within six years. The fine in Belgium is tiny: 1–25BFr. The penalty in Greece, again a small fine, is seldom imposed. The Italian Constitution defines voting as a 'civic duty' and voters believe that failure to vote, which used to be recorded on identification and work papers, may result in discrimination when seeking jobs (Powell 1980: 9).[6] For the first four sets of direct elections, turnout was on average 30 per cent lower when voting was not compulsory (55.3 per cent) than when it was (85.3 per cent). This finding is in line with, although of much greater magnitude than,

6.   I have taken voting in Italy to be non-compulsory throughout, since the constitution merely called voting a 'civic duty'. However, because the names of abstainers were published and the fact they had abstained was stamped on their certificates of good conduct prior to a change in the law in 1993, Blondel *et al.* (1997: 269, n. 1) analyse voting in Italy as compulsory.

Powell's findings, seeming to suggest there is something different about EP elections, at least in the minds of voters.

Table 6.3: The Effect of Compulsory Voting on Turnout

	Date	Mean Turnout	Standard deviation	Number of cases
Voting is not compulsory	1979	58.97	16.23	7
	1984	54.30	15.23	7
	1987	70.75	2.61	2
	1989	55.08	13.47	9
	1994	50.14	13.50	9
Total		55.34	14.26	34
Voting is compulsory	1979	90.15	1.77	2
	1981	78.60	0.00	1
	1984	86.03	7.83	3
	1989	86.00	5.53	3
	1994	82.83	10.28	3
Total		85.29	6.82	12

Turnout across the whole EU declined over time regardless of whether voting was compulsory or not.[7] The change might be partly the result of fewer simultaneous elections occurring: in 1994 only Luxembourg held national and European elections on the same day, whereas in previous elections one or two other States had held national elections on the same date.

What then has the impact of *simultaneous elections* been? This should be taken into consideration when analysing Luxembourg, where national and European elections are always scheduled to coincide, and elections elsewhere which have coincided with national elections. In some instances, European elections have been scheduled on the same day as a national election (usually general elections, but sometimes local elections across most or all of the country). This has been the case for Luxembourg each time and for the new Member States, Greece, Spain and Portugal, at the time of their first European elections. Spain is a slightly ambiguous case, since the first European elections coin-

---

7.   In the case of compulsory voting, part of the difference may be explained by the fact that turnout in Greece, which only joined the Community in 1981, is fairly low, despite the fact that voting is technically compulsory, and the mean turnout in countries where voting is compulsory fell by 4 per cent between 1979 and 1984.

cided with local elections in 13 of the 17 provinces. For the purpose of this analysis, this situation is taken to be analogous to simultaneity of national and European elections. The theoretical literature tends to ignore questions of simultaneity, but intuitively it would seem likely to foster higher voter turnout than might otherwise be the case in non-national elections. In fact, turnout has been 19.4 per cent higher when European elections have coincided with national elections.

Table 6.4: The Effect of Simultaneity on Turnout

	Date	Mean turnout	Standard deviation	Number of cases
Elections are not simultaneous	1979	62.94	20.41	7
	1984	61.04	19.16	9
	1989	57.57	17.64	9
	1994	55.75	17.89	11
Total		58.92	18.05	36
Elections are simultaneous	1979	76.25	17.89	2
	1981	78.60	0.00	1
	1984	88.80	0.00	1
	1987[a]	70.75	2.62	2
	1989	78.53	9.62	3
	1994	86.60	0.00	1
Total		78.36	9.51	10

a. The European Parliament coincided with regional elections in 13 out of Spain's 17 regions.

Only in Denmark have voters been offered a choice over the nature of European integration in all four EU-wide sets of European elections. If there were a relationship between turnout and *party/social cleavage links*, one would expect to find it in Denmark. Yet the disparity between turnout in national and European elections has been larger in Denmark than in any of the other Member States. This gives some superficial evidence that a choice over the nature of European integration does not increase participation, even where such a choice appears to fit patterns of support in the country concerned. However, the linkage between supporters or opponents of European integration and the factions which stand in European elections is not comparable with the traditional relationships between national political parties and social groups. Thus one could argue that even when voters have been offered a choice concerning the future of European integration, 'parties' at the European level remain remote from the citizens. Moreover, even in Denmark, voters have not been offered choices about the direction of integration, nor about questions of European public policy, but rather they have been asked to vote for or against European integration.

Turnout in national elections also differs greatly between Member States, ranging from 94.9 per cent in 1978 in Belgium, where voting is compulsory, and 88.7 per cent in 1997 in Denmark, where voting is not compulsory, to 68.5 per cent in Ireland in 1989 and 1992 and 63 per cent in Portugal in 1995. As in EP elections, compulsory voting leads to increased turnout in national elections, although only by 9.2 percentage points, considerably less than the impact of compulsory voting in European elections. Similarly, while the use of proportional representation in national elections yields higher turnout than plurality/ majoritarian systems, the effect (7.3 percentage points) is far less significant than in European elections. Differences in levels of turnout in European elections may therefore reflect differing *national patterns* of voter participation turnout. In most cases turnout within countries tends to follow similar patterns for national and EP elections: Germany, for example, has enjoyed fairly high levels of turnout in national and European elections even though voting is not compulsory, nor have European and national elections coincided in Germany.

While institutional differences *between* countries are of primary concern in understanding differential turnout between Member States, differences *within* countries for national and European elections are important in showing differences between national and European level elections. The most significant changes are in France where elections to the EP are held under PR but a two-ballot single member majoritarian system is used in national elections, and Italy where, as noted earlier, a single member plurality system was introduced for the 1994 national elections but a proportional system with five multi-member constituencies was retained for the European elections. The 1986 elections to the French *Assemblée Nationale* were held using a system of PR, but the traditional two-ballot system was reintroduced in 1988. This potentially gives further scope for considering the effects of the electoral system. It must be remembered, however, that some degree of voter sophistication is necessary for differences in the electoral system to have an impact on voting behaviour. To the extent that voters are aware of them, changes in electoral regulations over time and between national and European elections might be expected to result in shifts in turnout.[8]

In Germany, all the seats are allocated on a national basis and no MEPs are directly elected, in contrast to national elections which are fought on the basis of the additional member system. The impact of this difference is intuitively obvious: the additional member system yields proportional results, so the change is unlikely to increase turnout on the grounds that it increases proportionality; breaking the voter-representative link may have a disincentive effect. This seems to have been the case in France in 1994. Research by Blondel *et al.* (1997: 255-56) shows that many French non-voters cited the electoral system (PR with closed lists, offering voters no choice of candidate) as a major reason for abstaining.

In the other Member States, the changes are more in the nature of fairly minor adaptations of the systems used in national elections, generally regarding the number of constituencies, as already noted, or the quotas used to allocate seats between parties. In European elections most of the countries use the d'Hondt highest average system for allocating the seats.[9] That system favours smaller parties since it is easier for a party that has not yet been allocated a seat to win one than for a party to win a second one. This might be expected to reduce the 'wasted vote' syndrome and lead to higher turnout in European elections, other things being equal (which of course they are not). One caveat is that varying the rules for different elections might introduce an element of confusion which could itself reduce turnout.

The *nature of the body to be elected* is likely to prove significant in the context of European elections for three main reasons:

1. The EP is *sui generis*—it is the only directly-elected transnational parliament—and this in itself is likely to have an impact on the elections. The role of the European institutions is less

---

8.   One counter-example to this assumption is France, where the shift from a majoritarian to a PR system for EP elections seems to have had the effect of 'depressing turnout by distancing the candidates from the voters and by giving rise to confusion and to dissatisfaction with the electoral process' (Blondel *et al.* 1997: 265).

9.   The d'Hondt highest average system distributes unallocated seats by dividing the number of votes cast for each party (V) by the number of seats it has won (S) plus one (V/S + 1).

clear-cut than in most nation states and the EP does not necessarily enjoy the same acceptance or perform the same role as
national parliaments;

2. Perceptions that the EP is a weak institution might have a
   depressing effect on turnout;

3. Like Swiss federal elections, elections to the EP change little;
   they have had no impact on the Council of Ministers (the
   effective legislative body of the EU) nor, prior to changes
   under the Maastricht Treaty, did they have an effect on the
   composition of the Commission (the Union's *de jure* executive). Even under the provisions of the Treaty of Amsterdam,
   the links with the electorate are only indirect at best.

Points (2) and (3) lead to questions surrounding first and second-order
elections. For Reif and Schmitt (1980: 9), the fact that there is 'less at
stake' in European elections means that voters are less likely to be
willing to participate. In terms of the legislative powers of the
Parliament, the 'less at stake' hypothesis has become less valid over
time, but this does not negate the argument: if voters *perceive* the EP to
be a weak institution, this may still be reflected in the way they vote.
Similarly, the fact that European elections have no direct effect on
domestic politics may increase voters' reluctance to participate in them.

Turnout: The Impact of Attitudes to European Integration[10]

Differences in turnout in European elections between the Member
States can largely be seen to be the result of whether or not voting is
compulsory and whether European elections coincide with national
elections. While differences in the type of electoral system in force may
have an impact on turnout it is not possible to make any clear assertions
in this respect since Great Britain is the only Member State where no
form of proportional representation was used in the first four sets of
direct elections. The fact that turnout is generally much lower than in

10. Franklin, van der Eijk and Oppenhuis have challenged the sort of claims
made in this section, arguing that, 'Particularly noteworthy is the fact that EC-
related attitudes, preferences and orientations play no significant role in the
explanation of electoral participation in European elections, in contrast to the
findings of some earlier, less elaborate studies' (quoted in Blondel *et al.* 1997: 246).
Despite their scepticism it seems that attitudes do have a part to play in explaining
behaviour in EP elections.

national elections cannot be explained by such institutional factors, since the changes are relatively limited in most cases.

However, the *nature of the institution* being elected is of great importance in this regard. That European elections change little, at least in terms of executive formation and the political agenda, may well have a depressing effect on turnout. The *de jure* and *de facto* powers of the European Parliament are less important in this regard than the powers that voters and politicians *perceive* it to have. When direct elections were first held, the EP was a fairly weak institution and the idea that this contributed to low voter participation was credible. However, opinion poll evidence indicates that voters tend to believe the European Parliament has more powers than it actually has (Niedermayer 1990: 46). This is significant since it brings into doubt Reif's assertion that the European elections are in a second-order electoral arena: not only does the EP wield significant powers, as shown in Chapter 4, but voters also attribute considerable powers to it.

Nevertheless, by 1994, however, the European elections still had only a very limited and indirect *impact on executive formation at the European level*. Although the EP had been granted a right to approve the Commission under the provisions of the TEU, there was no clear mechanism for the results of the EP elections to have an impact on the choice of Commissioners. The key point is that the elections are not for the Commission, and nor does the Commission emerge from the directly elected Parliament. This does not mean that the composition of the Commission is not affected by the elections at all: the choice of nominees for the Commission by governments in Member States may reflect the results of the elections but this is by no means automatic or quantifiable. Certainly the choice of Jacques Santer in 1994 had nothing to do with the outcome of the 1994 elections. Thus there was little chance for voters to be made aware of the increased role of the EP in the formation of the Commission.[11]

In any case, it seems that the *lack of change at the national level* is a crucial factor in the low turnout in European elections. The elections do not lead directly to changes in national government; the European Parliament acts at the supranational level, with decisions made having

---

11. One positive implication of the resignation of the Commission in March 1999 could prove to be a heightened awareness of the EP and its role in the appointment of the Commission, leading, perhaps, to increased turnout in EP elections.

an impact only indirectly at the national level, as legislation is implemented in the Member States' legislatures. That the lack of resonance at the national level should have a detrimental effect on voter mobilization at the European level is indicative of the wider problems facing European democracy in terms of the weakness of any sense of European identity.

If turnout is affected by the fact that EP elections offer voters little choice on matters of European integration, since parties scarcely differ in their approaches to the nature and functions of European policies, one could predict that turnout would be low in European elections. The position is equivalent to a non-competitive situation where the evidence suggests that voters turn out in smaller numbers than in competitive elections. While it is difficult to prove such a hypothesis empirically, Denmark offers a useful case study. As discussed in the previous chapter, the political groupings fighting the European elections in Denmark are based on cleavages which emerged during the 1972 referendum on accession. Thus, while voters may choose to vote for particular national policy issues, they are also given the opportunity of voting on pro- and anti-European lines and, since the 1992 referendum, pro- and anti-Maastricht lines. Yet, as already shown, this choice does not seem to have helped raise turnout. The question of whether debates and choices over the future direction of European integration and European issues would result in higher public participation remains open; by early 1999, no such choices had been presented in any of the Member States.

Tied to the idea that it is national rather than European issues which can serve to arouse voters' awareness in elections is the further question of 'Europeanness' (Niedermayer 1990: 47). Niedermayer defines this in terms of whether voters in the Member States are in favour of European integration based on responses to *Eurobarometer* questions: 'Are you in general for or against efforts towards uniting Western Europe?', and 'Taking everything into consideration, would you say that (your country) has on balance benefited or not from being a member of the European Community?' As Table 6.6 indicates, in four of the countries where turnout in the 1994 European elections was low—Denmark, Ireland, The Netherlands and Portugal—the proportion of voters expressing the belief that their country had benefited from EU membership was well above the 47 per cent EU average. The United Kingdom was the only country with particularly low turnout where this was not the case: only 41 per cent of respondents felt that the UK had benefited from membership. Admittedly the Danes and British were less supportive of attempts to unite Western Europe than the average, although the Irish and Portuguese expressed above average support (see Table 6.5). These two sets of data imply that Niedermayer's concept of 'Europeanness' does not provide an adequate explanation of low voter turnout.

A final point to consider is voters' perceptions of the European Parliament. Intuitively one might expect turnout to be low if voters consider the European Parliament to be a relatively powerless institution. *Eurobarometer* evidence suggests that the British, the Dutch and the Danes are the least favourably impressed by the European Parliament; the Portuguese by contrast have been the most impressed, with the Irish fourth (Hofricher and Klein 1993: 10). These figures seem to offer one reason for low levels of participation: voters have a poor impression of the European Parliament, even though only the Danish media—and recently the British—have tended to portray it in a negative light (Hofricher and Klein 1993: 20). Additionally, the nature and scope of European identity should be considered in this context: irrespective of the role the EP plays, or is perceived to play, in the life of the EU, the weak sense of being European may influence participation in the electoral process and may prove to be a factor which discriminates between voters and non-voters in European elections.

There are two aspects of European identity, or the lack of it, to consider. The first is that attitudes towards the European Union and European integration may affect voters' decisions to participate. For voters who are hostile towards the idea of the European Union, there is the question of whether or not to vote in elections for a European institution if by so voting they may be seen to be legitimizing that institution (Heath *et al.* 1995: 7). The second is that if voters feel only a weak attachment to the European Union and only a weak sense of European identity, they are likely to be more reluctant to participate than they are in national elections. Both phenomena would serve to reduce turnout in European elections and also, as the next section demonstrates, affect which parties obtain support.

Results of European Elections: Cycle, Size, Novelty and Protest

In parliamentary or presidential systems when there is a change of government, those parties which form the new government or hold the

Table 6.5: Attitudes towards the Unification of Western Europe, Autumn 1994

Question: 'Are you in general for or against making efforts towards uniting Western Europe?'

	Very much for %	For to some extent %	Against to some extent %	Very much against %	No reply %
Belgium	19	59	12	4	6
Denmark	21	37	22	17	3
Germany	26	44	16	6	8
Greece	36	45	8	3	8
Spain	24	53	11	3	9
France	19	53	14	5	9
Ireland	27	50	7	3	13
Italy	31	54	4	2	9
Luxembourg	38	39	14	2	7
Netherlands	18	58	12	5	7
Portugal	37	39	7	4	13
UK	16	44	18	11	11
EU average	24	49	12	6	9

Source: *Eurobarometer Trends* 1974–94

Table 6.6: Benefits of EU membership, Spring 1994

Question: 'Taking everything into consideration, would you say that (your country) has on balance benefited or not from being a member of the European Union?'

	Benefited %	Not benefited %	No reply %
Belgium	49	27	24
Denmark	64	26	10
Germany	41	38	21
Greece	69	18	13
Spain	38	43	19
France	39	40	21
Ireland	81	11	8
Italy	55	23	22
Luxembourg	67	19	14
Netherlands	70	13	17
Portugal	70	23	8
UK	41	43	16
EU average	47	34	19

Source: *Eurobarometer Trends* 1974–94

presidency are self-evidently 'successful'.[12] European elections do not lead to a change of government at the European level, so the results are less easy to quantify. They do, however, affect the political balance in the European Parliament, which is increasingly important since many of the new powers the EP has gained over the years require an absolute majority of all MEPs to be passed. Thus the elections have arguably become more significant in that they can contribute to a change in the direction of policy-making, at least to a limited extent.

Reif has suggested that to see the impact of the elections on the European Parliament it is necessary to consider them in a transnational perspective. However, he argues that in order to understand the *causes* of the changes, one must look at the *national* results (Reif 1984b: 244). The 1994 elections confirm this statement: rather than transnational trends in voting behaviour it is easier to view the results as the sum of their national components. This in itself is indicative of the dominance of national factors in European elections; patterns of support do not seem to be related to transnational parties or party federations, but rather to domestic political conditions.

How, then, have the elections affected the composition of the European Parliament? This section considers the impact of the elections on the EP, examining trends within those results and noting the widely divergent patterns of support enjoyed by parties from the same party groups in the different Member States. It demonstrates the validity of Reif's claims that there is a correlation between the position in the national electoral cycle at which EP elections are held and the level of support for governing parties. Reif's assertions concerning the relatively strong support for small, new and opposition parties are assessed.

As Table 5.2 indicates, there was little change in the sizes of the largest party groups following the 1994 election. However, while they retained roughly the same number of seats as in the outgoing parliament, this was in the context of an enlarged membership.[13] Three main features of the incoming parliament were: a fragmentation of the party groups; the dominance of several groups by single national parties; and a shift away from the three transnational parties.

---

12. Although even then the analysis may not be so simple: governing parties may, for example, retain power but with a reduced majority.

13. As noted earlier, following complex negotiations to take the unification of Germany into consideration, the EP was enlarged by 49 seats at the time of the 1994 elections.

Table 6.7: Seats by Party Group and Country, 19 July 1994

	B	DK	D	Gr	E	F	Irl	I	L	NL	P	UK	*Total*
PES	6	3	40	10	22	15	1	18	2	8	10	63	198
EPP	7	3	47	9	30	13	4	12	2	10	1	19	157
ELDR	6	5	—	—	2	1	1	7	1	10	8	2	43
United Left	—	—	—	4	9	7	—	5	—	—	3	—	28
FE	—	—	—	—	—	—	—	27	—	—	—	—	27
EDA	—	—	—	2	—	14	7	—	—	—	3	—	26
Greens	2	1	12	—	—	—	2	4	1	1	—	—	23
ERA	1	—	—	—	1	13	—	2	—	—	—	2	19
EN	—	4	—	—	—	13	—	—	—	2	—	—	19
Non-attached	3	—	—	—	—	11	—	12	—	—	—	1	27
Total	25	16	99	25	64	87	15	87	6	31	25	87	567

Tables 6.8, 6.9 and 6.10 demonstrate how the overall result conceals the very different fortunes of the member parties of three transnational parties. The Socialist Group retained its numbers primarily because of the strength of the British Labour Party, which gained seventeen seats, offsetting the Spanish and French Socialists' losses of five and seven seats respectively.[14] The position of the Italian member parties was somewhat more complicated: they had four more representatives in the PES than at the start of the 1989–94 parliament, but this was largely due to the shift in January 1993 of the former Communist Party of the Democratic Left's (PDS) MEPs from the United European Left to the PES. The PDS lost six seats in 1994, while the Socialists fell from twelve to just two. Six additional seats for the Dutch Liberals and So-cial Liberals (VVD and D'66), giving the Dutch a quarter of the ELDR membership, and the British Liberal Democrats' first two elected MEPs, were partly counterbalanced by the loss of German represen-tation in the ELDR Group. The two Danish member parties of ELDR were successful, with the social liberals, *Det Radikale Venstre*, increas-ing their support by 5.7 per cent and gaining their first EP seat, and *Venstre* increasing its vote by 2.4 per cent and gaining an additional seat. And although *Det Radikale Venstre* had not used the ELDR Party manifesto in its election campaign, its MEP sat with the Group. The Belgian Liberal parties did not perform as well as they had hoped, but both the Flemish and Walloon parties won an extra seat nevertheless.

14. These figures are all based on the actual membership of the Parliament and are not weighted to take the enlargement of the Parliament into consideration.

Table 6.8: Votes for Member Parties of the ELDR Group: 1979–96*

Country	Member Party	1979 Votes %	1979 Seats	1984 Votes %	1984 Seats	1987 Votes %	1987 Seats	1989 Votes %	1989 Seats	1994 Votes %	1994 Seats	1995 Votes %	1995 Seats	1996 Votes %	1996 Seats
Austria	Liberal Forum													4.2	1
Belgium	Flemish Liberals and Democrats (VLD)	9.4	2	8.6	2			10.6	2	11.4	3				
	Liberal Reform Party (PRL)	6.9	2	9.4	3			7.2	2	9.0	3				
Denmark	Venstre	14.5	3	12.5	2			16.6	3	19.0	4				
	Det Radikale Venstre	0	0	0	0			2.8	0	8.5	1				
Finland	Centre Party													24.4	4
	Swedish People's Party													5.7	1
Germany	Free Democrats (FDP)	6.0	4	4.8	0			5.6	4	4.1	0				
Ireland	Independent	14.3	2	13.1	1			6.8	2	6.9	1				
Italy	Northern League	0	0	0	0			1.8	2	6.6	6				
	Radicals, Liberals and Republicans	9.9	8	9.5	8			4.4	4	3.0	3				
Luxembourg	Democratic Party (DP)	28.1	2	22.1	1			20.0	1	18.9	1				
Netherlands	Freedom and Democracy Party (VVD)	16.2	4	18.9	5			13.6	3	17.9	6				
	Democrats 66 (D'66)	9.0	2	2.3	0			5.9	1	11.7	4				
Portugal†	Social Democratic Party (PSD)					38.4	10	32.7	9	34.4	9				
Spain	Catalan Party					4.4	3	4.3	2	4.7	3				
Sweden	Centre Party (C)											7.2	2		
	Liberal Party (FpL)											4.8	1		
UK	Liberal Democrats	12.6	0	19.5	0			6.4	0	16.1	2				
Total Seats			29		22				35		46				

* France has been omitted because its ELDR MEP was elected on a joint list with other centre-right parties whose Members sit in other groups. Greece has been omitted since it has no ELDR MEPs. Germany has been included because it had a significant representation in the ELDR group in the 1979–84 and 1989–94 parliaments. † PSD MEP shifted to the EPP Group in November 1996.

The most dramatic changes in fortune among the EPP group parties were for the British Conservatives and Spanish Popular Party. The Popular Party's support almost doubled from 21.7 per cent in 1989 to 40.2 per cent in 1994, securing 13 more seats. The Conservatives lost 14 seats, although their support was only reduced by 7.3 per cent. This outcome reflects the nature of the British electoral system, which favours the largest party and in previous elections had helped the Conservatives. Although overall support for the German Christian Democrat parties actually fell by 0.7 per cent, the losses were sustained only by the Christian Social Union in Bavaria; support for its sister party, the CDU, rose by 0.7 per cent and the coalition thus won 15 extra seats.[15] The scandals which led to the breakdown of the Italian party system affected the Christian Democrats particularly badly, with the two Christian Democrat lists jointly winning 15 fewer seats than the single Christian Democrat list had done in 1989. Support for the Greek New Democracy party fell by 7.7 per cent, but this only led to the loss of one seat.

Following corruption scandals in Belgium, Spain and Italy, the Socialists in those countries all lost support compared with 1989, winning respectively two, five and ten seats fewer than in 1989. Although not tainted by these scandals, the Italian Party of the Democratic Left, whose members had joined the PES in January 1993, also suffered heavy losses (down 8.5 per cent and losing six seats). The German Social Democrats gained nine additional seats, due in the main to the allocation of eighteen new seats for Germany; their percentage votes fell from 37.3 per cent to 32.2 per cent. The vagaries of the British electoral system meant that a gain of just 2.6 per cent for the Labour Party gave it an additional seventeen seats.

The French parties of the centre-right—the Gaullist RPR and the UDF—lost five seats compared with the 1989 elections.[16] Although the RPR and UDF candidates fought on a single list using the EPP manifesto, only thirteen of the MEPs elected on that list opted to sit with the EPP, one sat with the ELDR group and the remaining fourteen sat in the nationalist European Democratic Alliance (EDA) and subsequently as part of the Union for Europe group (see Table 5.2). In the previous

15. The figures for Germany are complicated by the fact that the 1989 figures refer only to West Germany, while the 1994 figures refer to unified Germany.

16. This is comparing the combined results for the Centre/Veil and RPR/Giscardian lists of 1989 with the single centre-right list in 1994.

Table 6.9: Votes for Member Parties of the EPP Group: 1979–96*

Country	Member Party	1979 Votes %	1979 Seats	1981 Votes %	1981 Seats	1984 Votes %	1984 Seats	1987 Votes %	1987 Seats	1989 Votes %	1989 Seats	1994 Votes %	1994 Seats	1995 Votes %	1995 Seats	1996 Votes %	1996 Seats
Austria	People's Party (OeVP)															29.6	7
Belgium	Christian People's Party	29.5	7			19.8	4			21.1	5	17.4	4				
	Christian Social Party	8.2	3			7.6	2			8.1	2	6.9	2				
	Christian Social Party (German)	0	0			0	0			0	0	0.2	1				
Denmark	Conservative People's Party	14.0	2			20.8	4			13.3	2	17.7	3				
Finland	National Coalition Party															20.2	4
Germany	Christian Democratic Union	39.1	34			37.5	34			29.5	25	30.2	39				
	Christian Social Union	10.1	8			8.5	7			8.2	7	6.8	8				
Greece	New Democracy			31.3	8	38.1	9			40.4	10	32.7	9				
Ireland	*Fine Gael*	33.0	4			32.2	6			21.6	4	24.3	4				
Italy	Italian Popular Party (ex-CDs)	36.4	29			33.0	26			32.9	26	10.0	8				
Luxembourg	Christian Social People's Party (CSV)	36.1	3			34.9	3			34.9	3	31.4	2				
Netherlands	Christian Democrats	35.6	10			30.0	8			34.6	10	30.8	8				
Spain	Popular Party (PP)							24.7	17	21.7	15	40.2	28				
Sweden	Moderate Party													23.1	5		
UK	Conservatives	48.4	60			40.8	45			34.1	32	26.8	18				
	Official Ulster Unionist Party (OUP)	0.9	1			1.1	1			0.8	1	0.8	1				
Total Seats			161				149				142		135				

* The French and Portuguese centre-right parties have been omitted from this table since they have tended not to sit in a single group in the EP. The Portuguese PDS has been included in Table 6.8, since the party was a member of the ELDR party until November 1996. *Forza Italia*, many of whose members joined the EPP during the lifetime of the 1994–99 parliament, has also been excluded.

Table 6.10: Votes for Parties in the Group of the PES, 1979–96

Country	Member Party	1979 Votes %	1979 Seats	1981 Votes %	1981 Seats	1984 Votes %	1984 Seats	1987 Votes %	1987 Seats	1989 Votes %	1989 Seats	1994 Votes %	1994 Seats	1995 Votes %	1995 Seats	1996 Votes %	1996 Seats
Austria	Social Democratic Party															29.1	6
Belgium	Flemish Socialist Party (SP)	12.8	3			17.1	4			12.4	3	10.8	3				
	Walloon *Parti Socialiste* (PS)	10.6	4			13.3	5			14.5	5	11.3	3				
Denmark	Social Democrats	21.9	3			19.5	3			23.3	4	15.8	3				
Finland	Social Democrats															21.5	4
France	Socialists (PS)	23.5	22			20.8	20			23.6	22	14.5	15				
Germany	Social Democratic Party (SPD)	40.8	35			37.4	33			37.3	31	32.2	40				
Greece	*Pasok*			40.1	10	41.6	10			36.0	9	37.6	10				
Ireland	Labour	14.5	4			8.4	0			9.5	1	11.0	1				
Italy	Party of the Democratic Left	29.6	24			33.3	27			27.6	22	19.1	16				
	Socialist Party (PSI-AD)	11.0	9			11.2	9			14.8	12	1.8	2				
Luxembourg	Socialist Workers' Party (LSAP)	21.7	1			29.9	2			25.4	2	24.8	2				
Netherlands	Labour Party (PvdA)	30.4	9			33.7	9			30.7	8	22.9	9				
Portugal	Socialist Party (PS)							23.1	10	28.5	9	34.8	9				
Spain	Socialist Workers' Party (PSOE)							39.1	28	40.2	27	30.7	22				
Sweden	Social Democrats													28.1	7		
UK	Labour Party	31.6	17			36.5	32			40.1	45	42.7	62				
	SDLP	1.1	1			1.1	1			0.9	1	1.0	1				
Total Seats			132				155				201		198				

parliament, the Giscardians sat with the ELDR Group; after the 1994 elections most joined the EPP Group, leaving a lone French representative in the ELDR Group.[17] The EDA ended up with one additional French Member compared with the outgoing Parliament as well as an extra Irish Member and an extra Greek, while the three Centre Social Democrats (CDS) Members from Portugal sat with it for the first time. This situation changed following the merger in July 1995 of the EDA and *Forza Europa*, which led to the creation of the Union for Europe, and later with the defection of many *Forza* MEPs to the EPP Group.

Among the smaller groups, the Greens fell from 27 MEPs to 23, in marked contrast to 1989 when there seemed to be an incipient transnational trend towards ecology parties (Curtice 1989). However, there was a large increase in German representation from eight to 12. The Greens won their first EP seat in Luxembourg and their first two in Ireland. Elsewhere in the EU support for the Greens declined from the high of 1989. The change was especially notable in Great Britain where support fell from 15 per cent in 1989 to 3.1 per cent in 1994, although the vagaries of the British electoral system meant that this decline in support had no effect in the EP: even with 15 per cent in 1989 the Greens had not won a single seat.

Parties of the far right experienced very mixed fortunes. Italy's *Alleanza Nazionale*, formerly the MSI, won 11 seats compared with four in 1989. In Belgium *Vlaams Blok* gained one seat and the Wallonian National Front won its first seat. The French National Front won an additional seat, despite a 1.2 per cent decline in votes received. However, the German *Republikaner*, which had won six seats in 1989, did not reach the 5 per cent threshold in 1994 and so failed to win any seats.

Given that there appear to be so few transnational trends in support for particular parties, what other general features might have affected the fortunes of particular parties?

Governing Party Support
In line with Reif's predictions (1984b: 246) the results of the elections correlated well with the timing within the domestic electoral cycle: in the 1994 EP election governing parties in all the Member States bar

---

17. These results have not been incorporated into the tables or figures relating to the EPP since there is no clear way of assessing the relative levels of support for the UDF and RPR candidates, who were placed alternately on the rigid party list.

Italy performed less well than they had in the previous national election.[18] Plotting the change in percentage votes for governing parties compared with the previous national elections against the point in their respective electoral cycles, we can see that, in general, Reif's hypothesis holds for the 1994 election (see Figure 6.5).

The main exception to the idea that governing parties perform badly in mid-cycle was Belgium, where, despite corruption scandals, support for the ruling coalition fell by only four percentage points. This is primarily due to the fragmented nature of the ruling coalition and of Belgian politics as a whole. Of the four governing parties, only the Christian People's Party increased its vote, but the Flemish and Walloon Socialists and the Christian Social Party saw only slight declines in support. Nevertheless, this case highlights a point first shown by The Netherlands in 1979: where there are multi-party coalitions, gains and losses for the various ruling parties might cancel out (Reif 1985: 13).

Support for the Danish governing coalition appears rather low until two factors are taken into account. First, there was subsequently a change in government formation following the election held in September 1994, hence the low support for the governing party was indicative of a general rather than cyclical loss of support. (This factor can also explain the slight deviance in support for the Portuguese governing parties, with elections held in October 1995 leading to a change in government from the Social Democrats to the Socialists.) Secondly, the People's Movement and June Movement do not fight national elections and so their participation necessarily reduces support for other parties in EP elections. In Germany, support for the governing coalition fell primarily because of the long-run decline of the minor, but pivotal, coalition party, the FDP, which had performed uncharacteristically well in the 1990 general election. Thus it seems that positions in government and timing in the electoral cycle do have an important effect on the results of European elections, although the correlation is not exact and certainly works less well in states with coalition governments.

18. Here Luxembourg is omitted since the national and European elections were held simultaneously. The Netherlands have also been excluded because, although the general election had taken place in May, no government had been formed at the time of the EP elections.

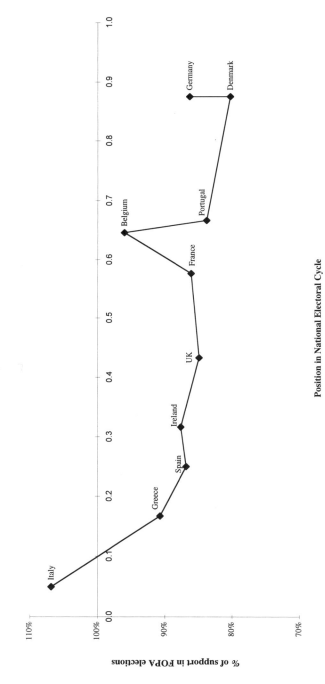

6.5 *Governing Party Support as a Function of the National Electoral Cycle**

Position in National Electoral Cycle

% of support in FOPA elections

* Luxembourg and the Netherlands have been omitted because at the time of the European elections no government was in place.

Large Party Support
Reif and Schmitt (1980: 17) also assert that large parties perform badly in second-order elections. Support for large parties (defined as those parties which won more than 15 per cent of the votes in the previous national election) certainly tended to fall at the 1994 EP elections (see Figure 6.6); however, the pattern was not particularly consistent. In Belgium support for large parties actually rose by 0.2 per cent, which can partly be explained by the fragmentation of the party system: only the Christian People's Party falls into Reif's large party category. Elsewhere support shifted by markedly different amounts: in Spain it fell by only 2.5 per cent, while in Denmark it fell by 18.4 per cent and in France by 18.6 per cent.

This measure is rather misleading because it includes the support for governing parties, whose support has already been demonstrated to fall in second-order elections. Looking only at large opposition parties a rather different picture emerges (see Figure 6.7). Mapping support against the point in the electoral cycle gives a virtual mirror image of Figure 6.5 which maps the governing parties' support. Only Ireland, where the sole large opposition party, *Fine Gael*, lost 0.2 per cent, and France, where the Socialists went down 4.7 per cent, seem to buck this trend. (Belgium is excluded as it has no large opposition parties. Luxembourg and The Netherlands are again excluded because no government had been formed by the time of the European elections.) The apparently disastrous outcome for Danish opposition parties is, like the loss of support for government parties, attributable to support for the anti-integration lists. The poor performance of the Italian PDS was due to the 'honeymoon' still enjoyed by the Berlusconi coalition. Thus, it seems that while governmental parties do typically perform less well in European elections than national first-order elections, the size of the party is of less importance.

Small, New and Extreme Party Support
Reif's hypothesis that small parties perform well in European elections was confirmed by the 1994 elections (the change in support being a mirror image of Figure 6.6). But there is no pattern of support for particular types of small party. As has already been argued, the Green parties saw very mixed fortunes in the 1994 elections, as did the parties of the far right.

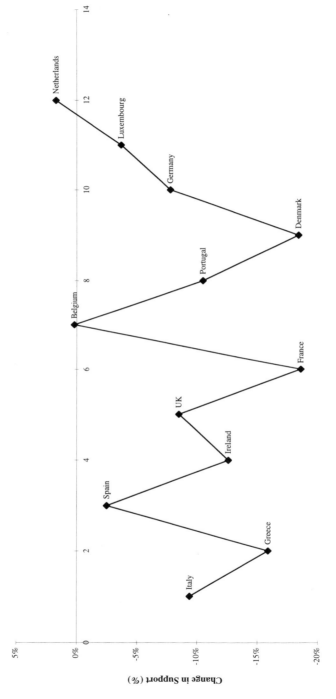

6.6 Change in Large Party Support as a Function of the National Electoral Cycle

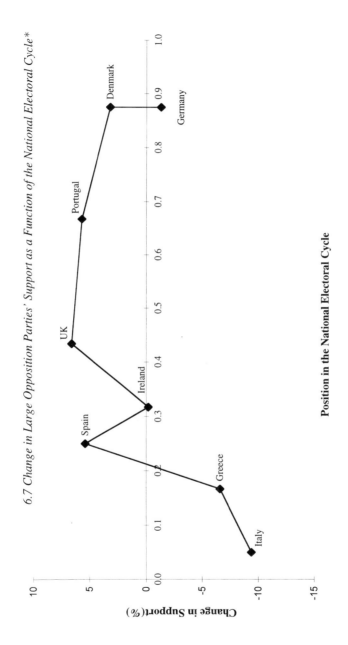

6.7 Change in Large Opposition Parties' Support as a Function of the National Electoral Cycle*

Position in the National Electoral Cycle

* Luxembourg and the Netherlands have been omitted because at the time of the European elections no government was in place. France has been omitted because the nature of cohabitation resulted in several major parties being involved in government. Belgium is not shown because there were no large opposition parties in 1994.

Small parties frequently serve as vehicles for protest, which may partly explain why they do well in second-order elections. Seeking a way to punish governments, voters cast their ballots for minor parties when they feel they can do so without causing a change of government. Such behaviour does not necessarily serve to predict defeat for the government at the following election: voters may either revert to traditional support regardless of whether the government has altered its course of action in any way, preferring the government to the minor parties; alternatively, the governing parties may have responded to the shock in the second-order elections and altered their behaviour. A further factor is the phenomenon of the 'wasted vote'. In national elections voters may decide not to vote for their first preference party or candidate because they feel that there is little chance of that party being successful, preferring instead to maximize their chance of achieving some representation (Blais and Carty 1991: 80). In second-order elections these voters may feel able to cast a vote which reflects their true party loyalty.

There is a large amount of overlap between new and small parties which perform well in second-order elections. Thus, in 1984 the Greens in Germany and the FN in France were both small and new. The FN also fulfilled another characteristic of successful parties: it is an extreme party. Yet these points cannot easily be quantified: it is relatively simple to look at the performance of small parties but, from a methodological perspective, harder to assess what all these parties stand for. In Greece 50 parties presented lists in the 1994 elections, and in Spain 37 (European Parliament 1994a, 1994b); inevitably lack of access to information on such a wide range of insignificant parties precludes a detailed analysis of all those that fielded candidates. In any case such an approach would be superfluous: only Italy and Belgium saw more than ten parties secure representation, the others ranging from seven for the United Kingdom and Denmark down to four for Germany, Luxembourg and Portugal.

Belgium offers the clearest support for Reif's hypothesis, with the Flemish extreme right party, *Vlaams Blok*, increasing its vote from 4.1 per cent to 7.8 per cent and gaining an extra seat, and the new Walloon National Front gaining its first seat. The Italian political situation was even more complicated. The proliferation of parties can largely be explained by the fact that they did not fight on common slates as had happened in the general election in March 1994. Although the *Alleanza*

Nazionale can plausibly be considered an anti-system party, its presence in the first government after the election would seem to vindicate its right to be considered as a pro-regime party. In fact, all parties in the Italian governing coalition fared well in the European elections, benefiting from a 'honeymoon period'. This hides the fact that most of the parties in the Italian party system of the 1990s were new and it was the *national* situation which had acted as the launching-pad for new parties.

France gives the clearest example of small and new parties performing well. The anti-Maastricht list, *L'Autre Europe*, won 12.3 per cent of the vote and 13 seats, and *Energie Radicale* 12 per cent and 13 seats. Both the Socialist Party, which held the presidency, and RPR/UDF parties, which held a parliamentary majority, performed especially badly.

Approaches to European Integration
The French case is particularly interesting because it raises a final question for analysis: how did attitudes towards European integration affect support for the parties? As already mentioned, there was a marked increase in 1994 in the number of parties fighting on an anti-European platform. However, while it is tempting to conclude that this might have reflected the start of a new 'European' cleavage, dividing those who favour further integration from those who do not, the evidence does not substantiate such a claim.

L'Autre Europe performed well in France, but its performance was matched by the strongly European *Energie Radicale*, which seems to imply that voters in France were seeking an alternative to the established parties rather than opposing European integration. The fact that the two centre-right parties, the UDF and the RPR, fought on a joint, nominally pro-European platform meant that those who were less keen on European integration were deprived of the opportunity specifically to vote for the party traditionally hesitant about integration, the RPR.

In Denmark support for anti-Maastricht lists rose from 18.9 per cent for the People's Movement Against the EC in 1989 to 25.5 per cent for the two anti-integration lists in 1994. Had the two parties fought on a single list they would have secured an additional seat. As it was, they failed to improve on the four seats won by the People's Movement in 1989. However, this was the only other case where support for anti-integration policies actually helped determine electoral success. Despite a high profile campaign and against earlier expectations, the *Bund Freier Burger* in Germany, led by Manfred Brunner, won only 1.1 per cent of the votes in that country. In Britain candidates fighting on an explicitly anti-European platform won about 3.5 per cent of the votes in the seats they fought. As they fought only 43 seats, however, the impact on the outcome was negligible (Butler and Westlake 1995: 319-20).

Conclusions

European elections up to 1999 saw few transnational tendencies. There were no signals to the Commission or to the Council of Ministers about what European voters wanted from the European Union. Indeed, more than anything else, the elections highlighted the point that it was premature to speak of a European electorate except in a technical sense.

While parties nominally fought as European parties, the reality was that the elections were perceived as contests between national players, and electors cast their votes accordingly. The results represented the sum of 12 national contests and depended largely on certain characteristics of those parties such as their size and whether they were in government or opposition.

This was particularly shown by the dominance of several of the groups by a few, or even just one, national parties. Apart from the three new groups, the membership of the EDA was over half French, a quarter of the ELDR's members were Dutch, while the PES was dominated by the British Labour Party. This situation was exacerbated by the lack of a common electoral system coupled with a wide disparity in the number of seats allocated to the Member States: both factors enabling some parties to wield a much greater influence in the groups and in the EP itself—for example, Spanish MEPs held three of the EP's 14 vice-presidencies in the 1994–99 parliament.

By 1994, the introduction of direct elections had not fostered a demonstrably transnational European party system. Moreover, apart from the PES, the EPP, the ELDR and the Greens whose membership was moderately well defined by party/federation membership, the groups were still typically coalitions which formed after the elections. The French Gaullists and Irish *Fianna Fáil* MEPs sat together in successive parliaments, but because the Gaullists favour a loose Europe of nation states, they have not run joint campaigns or had joint manifestos.

No cleavage on approaches to European integration emerged; where parties were internally divided in their approaches to European integration they generally tried to hide this by focusing on national issues (for example the Spanish Popular Party). Anti-European parties were only successful in France and Denmark; elsewhere the victorious parties elected were all broadly-speaking committed to continuing European integration.

7 |

Conclusions

> You asked me: 'Isn't the United States of Europe just a utopia?' I think
> that for any large human undertaking to succeed, there is always an ele-
> ment of a dream (Monnet 1972).

This book has outlined some of the dreams and nightmares surrounding
the creation of a European Parliament. As indicated in Chapter 2, in the
early postwar years there was no consensus about what integration
would entail or what its institutions should look like; even Jean Monnet
was unwilling to accept merely '*one* concept or *one* method' (Küsters
1989: 54). Rather, a complex set of ideas gave rise to the institutions of
the European Communities, including the Parliament. The Common
Assembly was not designed to be the legislative arm of a prototype
federal system. It was a gesture ensuring that the supranational High
Authority, which could act independently of the Member States in
certain policy sectors, could be held accountable for its actions, to a
body that was indirectly elected by the people.

Similarly, direct elections to the European Parliament were supported
for a variety of reasons, some idealist, some pragmatic. For federalists,
a directly-elected parliament added a necessary democratic aspect to
the new supranational state they hoped to create. Pluralists rejected the
idea of direct elections to a supranational parliament for precisely the
reason that led the federalists to favour them: the assumption that they
would give legitimacy to an institution above the national level. The
decision to introduce elections was eventually taken in the wake of a
prolonged period of Eurosclerosis, in the belief that elections and the
campaigns surrounding them would increase public support for
European integration, which had declined in the early 1970s.

For those federalists and others who demanded European elections,
there was no contradiction in holding supranational elections, which
they felt would simply resemble national elections, with European
parties emerging to fight on European issues. However, although

European political 'parties' have been created, the reality is far from the expectations. European political parties have not stood for something new and have done little to cut across national boundaries. Even where new parties have emerged in European elections, they have succeeded at the *national*, rather than the *European*, level. Thus, the success of Green parties in several Member States in the 1980s appears to have resulted from a convergence of national preferences rather than indicating the emergence of a transnational post-materialist party system. Within the European Parliament, the willingness of politicians to cooperate across national lines has frequently reflected a pragmatic desire to achieve certain specific results, rather than a shift towards new transnational cleavages.

Nor by 1994 had European elections fulfilled the Commission's hopes that they would give 'the peoples of Europe an interest in the destinies of the Community' (Rey 1970). With limited policy differences between the main European party groupings, voters were not offered any clear choices, either on the future development of the European Union or on specific public policy issues. The lack of polarity in the European party system coupled with the limited media coverage of the EP and its elections may have contributed to the low turnout in European elections, which suggests that, in contrast to expectations, elections have done little to arouse popular support for the EU. Admittedly awareness of the European Parliament typically rose in the months preceding elections, but such shifts were weak and temporary. Only in spring 1984 did awareness of the European Parliament rise significantly, with 75 per cent of respondents replying positively to the *Eurobarometer* question, 'Have you recently seen or heard in the papers, or on the radio or TV, anything about the European Parliament, that is the parliamentary assembly of the European Community?' By Autumn 1986 this figure had dropped to its lowest point since *Eurobarometer* first asked the question in 1977, with a mere 42 per cent answering in the affirmative.[1]

Analysis
The durability of the nation state has undoubtedly hindered moves towards the type of European polity favoured by federalists. Indeed

---

1.   These figures must be used with caution, since the 1984 figures refer to the then ten members of the EC, while the 1986 figures include Spain and Portugal as well (*Eurobarometer Trends 1974–91* Table B8).

some authors such as Milward (1992) and Chryssochoou (1994: 6-7) have argued that the process of European integration has led to a strengthening of the nation state. The Gaullists' emphasis on national politics seems to reflect the nature of loyalties, as predicted by Monnet, who:

> supposed that the main obstacle in the way of the achievement of peaceful cooperation would be this tendency of politicians to think in nation-state categories (Küsters 1989: 49).

This point is significant: national elites have been reluctant to recognize the shift in the locus of power. In terms of European elections this has meant that political parties have been unwilling to campaign vigorously, in turn making it much harder to interest voters in the European Union. Moreover, given the nature of EU decision-making where, even after Maastricht, key decisions have been made in the Councils of Ministers and the European Council, with treaty reforms also subject to ratification in the individual Member States, there appear to be few incentives for national elites to shift their attention to the European level, as they ultimately still determine policy outcomes. As Lindberg (1963: 9) points out:

> Actors with political power in the national community will restructure their expectations and activities only if the tasks granted to the new institutions are of immediate concern to them, and only if they involve a significant change in the conditions of the actors' environment.

The problem for those who wish to see democratic decision-making shifted to the European level is that national politicians are keen to preserve their powers and so refuse to recognize the extension of powers to the European level, resulting in minimal change to the policy-making environment. Thus ambitious young politicians, especially in Britain, remained more likely to go into national than European politics and perpetuate the desire to retain national control on decision-making procedures (Westlake 1994c: 270). The situation has changed over the years, however, as shown by the cases of Joyce Quin, who was a Labour MEP prior to becoming an MP and subsequently Minister for Europe, and Gijs de Vries, the leader of the ELDR group in the EP from 1994–98 when he was given a position in the new Dutch administration. Other politicians move apparently effortlessly between the EP and national government, but there remains a vestige of truth in the idea that MEPs are older politicians whose national careers are over or younger politicians who view membership as a stepping stone to national office.

The apparent dismissal of the EP by national politicians (especially backbenchers whose experience of European decision-making remains necessarily limited) belies the reality: significant decisions are taken at the European level over which national parliamentarians may have no control and national governments little influence. Indeed, as previous chapters have shown, this loss of national control led to increased powers for the European Parliament, culminating with the changes arising from in the Treaty of Amsterdam. Thus the idea that power remains at the national level is untenable. However, one major difference between the national and European levels persists: as mentioned in Chapter 3, in most EU countries, the government emerges from the parliament, hence parliamentary elections also serve to create the executive and parliamentarians can make or break governments. European Parliament elections, by contrast, have no impact on the composition of the Council of Ministers and, as of early 1999, have had only a very remote impact on the College of Commissioners, giving voters little incentive to participate.

The situation changed slightly under the provisions of the Maastricht Treaty, with Parliament being granted the right of consultation over the incoming Commission. The provisions of the Treaty of Amsterdam, due to be used for the first time for the confirmation of the Prodi Commission in summer 1999 go even further, codifying in the Treaty framework some of the practices already adopted by the EP in its Rules of Procedure following Maastricht. These changes apparently offer considerable scope for MEPs to influence the composition of the Commission. Since the EP has been granted the right to vote on the nominee for the Commission Presidency, the dominant force in the incoming Parliament could veto a nominee not of the same political persuasion. MEPs did not take the opportunity to vote against Jacques Santer's candidature in 1994, largely because of pressure exerted by national political parties. At that time the Parliament's vote on the President was not grounded in the Treaty but only in its own Rules of Procedure, so arguably carried less weight than it would after the Treaty of Amsterdam, although Santer had said he would withdraw his candidature if the vote went against him. The fact that the initial nomination of the President comes from the Council still gives national leaders considerable leverage over their MEPs. A more likely change arising from the Treaty of Amsterdam is that the EP would exert some pressure on the Presidential candidate to ensure the political balance of the College of Commissioners would reflect the political balance of the Parliament. Given that the first four sets of European elections saw electors vote against national governing parties, such a development could well lead to a situation where the political complexion of the Commission and the Parliament were in opposition to that of the Council, potentially leading to increased difficulty in decision-making.

Such a shift would help overcome a further problem faced in the European Union: the lack of an 'opposition'. Most MEPs are in favour of further European integration and are obliged to work consensually by the majority requirements for much EU legislation, and vote on draft legislation on that basis. This means that voters have had little choice in European elections (Weiler 1992: 33). Although the situation altered somewhat in 1994 with the emergence of Euro-sceptic party lists in some Member States, Shepherd's (1975: 234) analysis prior to the first European elections that one vital element of liberal democracy—political opposition—was missing from the European enterprise remained valid after four sets of elections.

This characterization of European politics is the inevitable result of the principles underlying the creation of the original Communities: rational, technocratic decision-making. The belief of Monnet and others was that the passion could be taken out of politics by using agencies to solve 'technical' problems. Initial proposals for European integration paid little attention to the publics, with the Common Assembly created as a way of curbing the powers of the supranational High Authority.

Federalists, who had argued strongly for a European Assembly, assumed public support for integration in the years immediately following the Second World War. When that support did not seem to be forthcoming, they argued that elections would help to create and to mobilize support for integration. Federalists believed that by introducing elections it would be possible to create a supranational polity with democratic underpinnings. However, such assumptions fail to appreciate the nature of public opinion. In reality citizens as political beings are motivated by many different forces, including both rational and non-rational factors. Thus many will retain apparently non-rational loyalties to the nation state because of past benefits and symbols. In the words of Karl Deutsch (1953: 152):

> Only if nationality is valued; if it is seen as a winning card in the social
> game for prestige, wealth or whatever else may be the things culturally
> valued at that time and place; or if it fulfils a need in the personality
> structure which individuals have developed in that particular culture—or
> at least valued for lack of any more promising opportunities—only then
> does it seem probable that consciousness of nationality will strengthen
> its development.

By the late 1990s such conditions for the development of a European identity remained rather distant. While it is, of course, possible to have multiple identities—someone from Bonn would have little difficulty in seeing himself as a citizen of Nordrhein-Westphalen, a German and a European—few would see being European as their sole identity.

European nation states typically gained a sense of national identity both from perceptions of a common external threat and from certain symbols of statehood—for example a flag, head of state and great monuments. The EU lacks symbols of statehood and thus is deprived of one method by which states have deliberately strengthened ideas of national identity (Wallace 1991: 66-70). Nor does the EU have the opportunity of fostering affective attachment by inventing national traditions and histories, since there is not a European equivalent of a state education system which could set a European curriculum.

The EU is not a state, but rather, in the words of William Wallace, a system of 'government without statehood' (Wallace 1996). Both the technocratic administrators and the member governments have ensured that the EU does not acquire the symbols of statehood, although a flag and anthem have belatedly been adopted. Moreover, one of the most potent forms of national symbolism, a national defence force, is lacking in the European Union. Thus several opportunities for increasing affective attachment are absent in the European context. Whether the Euro will provide such a focus of attachment in the Member States which have adopted it remains an open question.

The institutional framework of the EU after the Treaty of Amsterdam continues to reflect the tensions present when the three European Communities were created. The Commission, Court of Justice and the Parliament are clearly supranational, the Council of Ministers tends towards an intergovernmental approach, but with some concessions to majority voting, while the European Council operates on an intergovernmental basis. Coupled with different procedures in the three pillars of the Union, this situation leads to obscure and inefficient decision-making. There is little to inspire citizens, who can see few direct benefits from European integration, to shift their loyalties from the national or sub-national to the European level. Indeed, despite the introduction of direct elections and repeated treaty reform, Scheingold's analysis (1971: 389) remains pertinent:

> The available evidence, while once again inconclusive, suggests that the European Communities are not presently structured to promote a more active society. Their technocratic orientation and indirect institutions imply limited participation... The more fundamental problems are that: 1) the institutions are designed to minimize rather than maximize participation...

The citizens are entitled to vote, but only the most well-informed have any idea how their votes can affect the outcome of European legislation. The experience of increased EP powers through the co-decision procedure introduced by the Maastricht Treaty may have had some impact, but that will only be seen with the 1999 elections; the implications of the Treaty of Amsterdam remain to be seen.

At this point it is helpful to refer back to Michel Debré's (see p. 44 above) sceptical remarks about direct elections: are there really only national realities, or can European elections confer legitimacy? As Weiler (1992: 19) points out, 'democracy' and 'legitimacy' are not interchangeable: elections may not make a regime legitimate; a legitimate regime may not be democratic, although he does point out that 'it would be difficult for non-democratic government structure or political system to attain or maintain legitimacy in the West'. Weiler (1992: 19) rightly asserts that while legal legitimacy is attained if all the relevant laws of a state are fulfilled, a further aspect of legitimacy, 'social legitimacy' ('broad societal acceptance of the system') must also be considered.

The European Union enjoys formal legitimacy, but arguably lacks social and/or political legitimacy. No matter how democratic the institutions of such a new polity, some time will be needed before it acquires social legitimacy. This problem is compounded in the case of transnational elections: the level of government is even further removed from the citizen than are national governments. Voters thus have even less chance of affecting policy outcomes than at the national level. However, the trade-off is that they are influencing a larger political arena which is desirable in an interdependent world (Dahl 1994).

Using Lindberg and Scheingold's analysis of popular support, it appears that 'systemic support' is lacking in the European Union.

Lindberg and Scheingold categorized public attitudes in terms of 'identitive' and 'systemic' support. Identitive support is defined as the '"horizontal" interaction among the broader publics of the system', while systemic support refers to '"vertical" relations between the system and the publics' (Lindberg and Scheingold 1970: 40). Pluralists like Deutsch, they claim, 'view the growth of mutual identification among peoples as the defining characteristic of integration' (Lindberg and Scheingold 1970: 39). Lindberg and Scheingold themselves argued that systemic support was more useful when considering the European Community. This approach seems eminently reasonable: the greater the popular support for a system, the greater its legitimacy and the better its chances of success.

Whereas federalists assumed that loyalties and identities could simply be shifted to the supranational level, functionalists took a more realistic view of the situation, arguing that as people saw the benefits of supranational activity they would begin to identify more closely with the supranational or technocratic institution. This rational view of support fits Lindberg and Scheingold's definition of 'utilitarian' support, which is based on 'some perceived and relatively concrete interest' (Lindberg and Scheingold 1970: 40). However, functionalism ignores a further aspect of support: affective attachment, which 'seems to indicate a diffuse and perhaps emotional response to some of the vague ideals embodied in the notion of European unity' (Lindberg and Scheingold 1970: 40). It is this aspect of support which remains firmly located at the national level.

The emergence and consolidation of the nation state in the nineteenth and twentieth centuries offers some useful, but salutary, parallels with international integration. Some have argued that nations must precede states (Foltz 1963: 118). According to this view of the creation of political communities, the lack of a distinctive European identity would make it very difficult, if not impossible, to form a European polity. However, other writers including Gellner and Hobsbawm claim that nations have been created by states, not the other way round (Ludwig 1993: 63). Thus it appears that if the political leaders of the member governments and the Community institutions were sufficiently committed to fostering European integration they could attempt to make European publics aware of the importance of the EU.

Integration is not an automatic occurrence. Rather, as Monnet (1972) argued, 'necessity must lead people to unite' (my translation). In the early years of European integration, there were compelling reasons for unification; after 1989 they were significantly reduced. Institutions may persist once the original rationale for their existence has vanished (just as differences between political parties may persist after the social cleavages which led to their creation have vanished), but it is not certain that support for European integration is so easy to secure now that many of the factors leading to the creation of the EC have gone. The demise of the 'evil empire' and the transformation of Germany into a 'normal' state following unification reduce the apparent necessity for European states to integrate.

Although the economic arguments of interdependence constitute an even stronger reason for European integration in 1999 than they did in 1945, such arguments do not have the same emotive force as external security threats. The presence of affective systemic and identitive attachments could bridge the gap in this situation and give continued support to European integration even when the perceived benefits or 'need' decline. The alternative scenario is that after a period of beneficial integration the component states revert to independent action. Here the example of the villager in Ghana given by Fred Hayward (1971: 335) offers a parallel for Europe:

> ...it [national integration] was useful for independence, but now that the tribes have come together to free the country from foreign domination, it is time to revert to the individual tribes as the fundamental authority.

In other words, without sufficient support a community may wither.

Greater emphasis on the achievements of European integration, coupled with clarification of the various legislative functions leading to more efficient policy outcomes and coverage of the EP's role in the appointment and scrutiny of the European Commission, could help increase 'utilitarian systemic' support for the European Union. Here the EP's vote of confirmation on Romano Prodi at the final plenary session before the 1999 elections could serve as a useful tool for increased coverage of the EP and perhaps lead citizens to think that their votes can affect matters at the European level, in turn leading to increased participation in the elections. Moreover, if we accept that utilitarian support might lead to affective attachment, then the prognosis for involvement in subsequent European elections should be positive.

In a system where the locus of decision-making was obvious, there would be an incentive for national politicians to acknowledge the shift in the balance of power away from national parliaments. This in turn could lead to a greater focus on European election campaigns by the media and by politicians, which would help foster a sense of affective attachment among the voters. Assuming that this clarification of powers would entail a recognition of a clearly federal EU, the logical corollary would be a written constitution going beyond the existing Treaties. Such a constitution would have to be 'sold' to the peoples of Europe, in marked contrast to the Treaty on European Union. Much information and education would be necessary before such an option would be acceptable to a majority of voters, yet without such changes, the EU will find it increasingly difficult to function and its democratic credentials will remain in doubt. Although the Treaty of Amsterdam alleviated the problem to the extent of increasing the EP's powers of co-decision, hence reducing the democratic deficit, it did little to reduce the complexity and opaqueness of Union decision-making.

If European leaders were to take the initiative and accept far-reaching reforms, coupled with the measures necessary to convince the voters of the desirability of these changes, then they might move one step closer to a European Union based on democratic principles. These changes could most easily be achieved by a concerted media campaign actively supported by politicians. In conclusion, the analysis and advice put forward by Hagen Schulze (1992: 90) seems appropriate:

> 'Europe' must exist first of all in the minds of the people if it is to become a political reality. That is the task of the chosen few who have access to the media and who exert influence via the press and party and who are able to define certain fundamental concepts (my translation).

Regardless of whether nations precede states or the other way round, and of whether utilitarian support precedes affective attachment, without some sense of systemic support for the European Union, elections will not fulfil the expectations of their progenitors. The expansion of powers under the Treaties of Maastricht and Amsterdam mark a major advance in institutional terms, but will only help to create affective attachment to the extent that European elites—politicians, at the national as well as the European level, and journalists—make the citizens of Europe aware of such changes.

Statistical Appendix

For all tables in the Appendix, figures have been rounded. Unless otherwise indicated, sources are: European Parliament (1994b, 1994c, 1994d); Keesing's (1995, 1996, 1997, 198); and Institute for Democracy and Electoral Studies (1999).

Turnout in Elections

Belgium

	1978 %	1979 %	1980 %	1984 %	1985 %	1987 %	1989 %	1992 %	1994 %	1995 %
National elections	94.9	n/a	94.6	n/a	93.6	93.3	n/a	92.0	n/a	91.1
European elections	n/a	91.4	n/a	92.1	n/a	n/a	90.7	n/a	90.7	n/a

Denmark

	1977 %	1979 %	1981 %	1984 %	1987 %	1988 %	1989 %	1990 %	1994 %	1998 %
National elections	88.7	85.6	83.2	88.4	86.8	75.8	n/a	83.0	n/a	86.0
European elections	n/a	47.8	n/a	52.3	n/a	n/a	46.2	n/a	52.5	n/a

France

	1974 %	1978 %	1979 %	1981 %	1984 %	1986 %	1988 %	1989 %	1993 %	1994 %	1997 %
National elections	84.3	82.8	n/a	81.1	n/a	78.1	81.3	n/a	69.0	n/a	68.0
European elections	n/a	n/a	60.7	n/a	56.7	n/a	n/a	48.7	n/a	52.7	n/a

Germany

	1976 %	1979 %	1980 %	1983 %	1984 %	1987 %	1989 %	1990 %	1994 %	1998 %
National elections	90.7	n/a	87.9	89.1	n/a	84.3	n/a	77.8	79.1	82.3
European elections	n/a	65.7	n/a	n/a	56.8	n/a	62.3	n/a	60.1	n/a

Greece

	1981 %	1984 %	1985 %	1989 %	1990 %	1993 %	1994 %	1996 %
National elections	78.6	n/a	83.8	84.5	83.2	81.5	n/a	76.3
European elections	78.6	77.2	n/a	79.9	n/a	n/a	71.2	n/a

Ireland

	1977 %	1979 %	1981 %	1982 %	1984 %	1987 %	1989 %	1992 %	1994 %	1997 %
National elections	76.3	n/a	76.2	73.8	n/a	73.4	68.5	68.5	n/a	66.1
European elections	n/a	63.6	n/a	n/a	47.6	n/a	68.3	n/a	44.0	n/a

Italy

	1976 %	1979 %	1983 %	1984 %	1987 %	1989 %	1992 %	1994 %	1996 %
National elections	93.2	90.4	89.0	n/a	90.5	n/a	83.2	86.1	82.9
European elections	n/a	84.9	n/a	83.4	n/a	81.0	n/a	74.8	n/a

Luxembourg

	1979 %	1984 %	1989 %	1994 %
National elections	88.9	88.8	92.1	88.3
European elections	88.9	88.8	87.4	86.5

The Netherlands

	1977 %	1979 %	1981 %	1982 %	1984 %	1986 %	1989 %	1994 %	1998 %
National elections	88.0	n/a	87.1	80.6	n/a	85.8	80.2	78.3	73.2
European elections	n/a	57.8	n/a	n/a	50.6	n/a	47.2	35.6	n/a

Portugal

	1987 %	1989 %	1991 %	1994 %	1995 %
National elections	72.6	n/a	68.2	n/a	66.8
European elections	72.6	51.2	n/a	35.6	n/a

Source of 1995 figure: Keesing's (1995: 40789)

Spain

	1986 %	1987 %	1989 %	1993 %	1994 %	1996 %
National elections	70.8	n/a	69.7	77.3	n/a	78.0
European elections	n/a	68.9	54.6	n/a	59.6	n/a

Source for 1996 figures: Keesing's (1996: 41008)

United Kingdom

	1979 %	1983 %	1984 %	1987 %	1989 %	1992 %	1994 %	1997 %
National elections	76.3	72.8	n/a	75.4	n/a	77.7	n/a	71.6
European elections	32.3	n/a	32.6	n/a	36.2	n/a	36.4	n/a

Source for 1997 figures: Keesing's (1997: 41647).

Election Results, 1979–

Belgium: Votes

Party	EP group	European election results				National results	
		1979 %	1984 %	1989 %	1994 %	1991 %	1995 %
Flemish Socialist Party (SP)	PES	12.8	17.1	12.4	10.8	12.0	12.6
Walloon *Parti Socialiste* (PS)	PES	10.6	13.3	14.5	11.3	13.5	11.9
Christian People's Party (CVP)	EPP	29.5	19.8	21.1	17.0	16.8	17.2
Christian Social Party (PSC)	EPP	8.2	7.6	8.1	6.9	7.7	7.7
Flemish Liberals & Democrats (VLD)	ELDR	9.4	8.6	10.6	11.4	12.0	13.1
Liberal Reform Party (PRL)	ELDR	6.9	9.4	7.2	9.0	8.1	10.3
Volksunie (VU)	ERA	6.0	8.5	5.4	4.4	5.9	4.7
Agalev	Green	1.4	4.3	7.6	6.7	4.9	4.4
Ecolo	Green	2.0	3.9	6.3	4.8	5.1	4.0
Vlaams Blok	NA	0.7	1.3	4.1	7.8	6.6	7.8
Christian Social Party (German)	EPP	—	—	—	0.2	—	—
National Front	NA	—	—	—	2.9	—	2.3
Others		12.5	6.1	3.0	6.9	6.7	

Source: Keesing's (1995: 40559)

Belgium: Seats

	1979	1984	1989	1994
Flemish Socialist Party (SP)	3	4	3	3
Walloon *Parti Socialiste* (PS)	4	5	5	3
Christian People's Party (CVP)	7	4	5	4
Christian Social Party (PSC)	3	2	2	2
Flemish Liberals & Democrats (VLD)	2	2	2	3
Liberal Reform Party (PRL)	2	3	2	3
Volksunie (VU)	1	2	1	1
Agalev	—	1	1	1
Ecolo	—	1	2	1
Vlaams Blok	—	—	1	2
Christian Social Party (German)	—	—	—	1
National Front	—	—	—	1
Others	2	—	—	—

Denmark: Votes

Party	EP group	European election results				National results	
		1979 %	1984 %	1989 %	1994 %	1994 %	1998 %
Social Democrats	PES	21.9	19.5	23.3	15.8	34.6	36.0
People's Movement Against the EU	I-EN	20.9	20.8	18.9	10.3	n/a	n/a
Conservative People's Party	EPP	14.0	20.8	13.3	17.7	15.0	8.9
Venstre	ELDR	14.5	12.5	16.6	19.0	23.2	24.0
Socialist People's Party	PES	4.7	9.2	9.1	8.6	7.3	7.5
Centre Democrats		6.2	6.6	7.9	0.9	2.8	4.3
Progress Party		5.8	3.5	5.3	2.9	6.4	2.4
Det Radikale Venstre	ELDR	—	—	2.8	8.5	4.6	3.9
June Movement	I-EN	—	—	—	15.2	n/a	n/a
Others		12.0	7.1	2.8	1.1	6.1	11.0

Source: Keesing's (1998: 42151)

Denmark: Seats

	1979	1984	1989	1994
Social Democrats	3	3	4	3
People's Movement Against the EU	4	4	4	2
Conservative People's Party	2	4	2	3
Venstre	3	2	3	4
Socialist People's Party	1	2	1	1
Centre Democrats	1	1	2	—
Progress Party	1	—	—	—
Det Radikale Venstre	—	—	—	1
June Movement	—	—	—	2
Others	1	—	—	—

France: Votes

Party	EP Group	European election results				National elections	
		1979 %	1984 %	1989 %	1994 %	1993 %	1997 %
Socialists (PS)	PES	23.5	20.8	23.6	14.5	19.2	23.4
UDF/RPR joint list	EPP/ELDR	—	43.0	—	25.6	—	—
RPR/Giscardian list		—	—	28.9	—	—	—
Centre/Veil list		—	—	8.4	—	—	—
RPR	UFE	16.3	—	—	—	20.4	15.7
UDF	EPP	27.6	—	—	—	19.1	14.2
L'Autre Europe	I-EN	—	—	—	12.3	—	—
Energie Radicale	ERA	—	—	—	12.0	—	—
Front National	NA	1.3	11.0	11.7	10.5	12.5	14.9
Communist Party (PCF)	EU/NGL	20.5	11.2	7.7	6.9	9.1	9.9
Greens		4.4	3.4	10.6	4.9	4.0	6.8
Others		6.3	10.7	9.1	13.3	15.7	15.1

Source: Keesing's (1997: 41694)

France: Seats

	1979	1984	1989	1994
Socialists (PS)	22	20	22	15
UDF/RPR joint list	—	41	—	28
RPR/Giscardian list	—	—	26	—
Centre/Veil list	—	—	7	—
RPR	15	—	—	—
UDF	25	—	—	—
L'Autre Europe	—	—	—	13
Energie Radicale	—	—	—	13
Front National	—	10	10	11
Communist Party (PCF)	19	10	7	7
Greens	—	—	9	—
Others	—	—	—	—

Germany: Votes

Party	EP Group	European election results				National elections	
		1979 %	1984 %	1989 %	1994 %	1994 %	1998 %
Social Democratic Party (SPD)	PES	40.8	37.4	37.3	32.2	36.4	40.9
Christian Democratic Union (CDU)	EPP	39.1	37.5	29.5	30.2	34.2	28.4
Christian Social Union (CSU)	EPP	10.1	8.5	8.2	6.8	7.3	6.7
Free Democrats (FDP)		6.0	4.8	5.6	4.1	6.9	6.2
Party of Democratic Socialism(PDS)		—	—	—	4.7	4.4	5.1
Die Grüne	Green	3.2	8.2	8.4	10.1	7.3	6.7
Republikaner		—	—	7.1	3.9	1.9	1.8
Others		0.8	3.6	3.9	6.2	1.1	3.0

Sources: Marsh (1994); Keesing's (1998: 42509).

Germany: Seats

	1979	1984	1989	1994
Social Democratic Party (SPD)	35	33	31	40
Christian Democratic Union (CDU)	34	34	25	39
Christian Social Union (CSU)	8	7	7	8
Free Democrats (FDP)	4	—	4	—
Die Grüne	—	7	8	12
Republikaner	—	—	6	—
Others	—	—	—	—

Greece: Votes

Party	EP group	European election results				National elections	
		1981 %	1984 %	1989 %	1994 %	1993 %	1996 %
Pasok	PES	40.1	41.6	36.0	37.6	46.9	41.5
New Democracy	EPP	31.3	38.1	40.4	32.7	39.3	38.1
Left Coalition & Progress		—	—	14.3	—	—	—
Communist Party of Greece (KKE)	EU/NGL	12.8	11.6	—	6.3	4.5	5.6
Left Alliance (SYN)	EU/NGL	5.3	3.4	—	6.3	—	5.1
Progress		1.2	—	—	—	—	—
Political Spring	UFE	—	—	—	8.7	4.9	2.9
Centre Right Alliance (DIANA)		—	—	1.4	2.8	—	—
EPEN		—	2.3	1.2	—	—	—
Kodiso		4.2	—	—	—	—	—
Others		4.7	3.0	6.7	5.6	4.4	6.8

Source: Keesing's (1996: 41293)

Greece: Seats

	1981	1984	1989	1994
Pasok	10	10	9	10
New Democracy	8	9	10	9
Left Coalition & Progress	—	—	4	—
Communist Party of Greece (KKE)	3	3	—	2
Left Alliance (SYN)	1	1	—	2
Progress	1	—	—	—
Political Spring	—	—	—	2
Centre Right Alliance (DIANA)	—	—	1	—
EPEN	—	1	—	—
Kodiso	1	—	—	—

Ireland: Votes

Party	EP Group	European election results				National elections	
		1979 %	1984 %	1989 %	1994 %	1992 %	1997 %
Fianna Fáil	UFE	34.7	39.2	31.5	35.0	39.1	39.3
Fine Gael	EPP	33.0	32.2	21.6	24.3	24.5	27.9
Labour	PES	14.5	8.4	9.5	11.0	19.3	10.2
Greens	Green	—	0.5	3.8	7.9	1.4	2.8
Independent	ELDR	14.3	13.1	6.8	6.9	—	—
Progressive Democrats		—	—	12.0	6.5	4.7	4.7
Democratic Left		—	—	7.5	3.5	2.8	2.5
Others			3.5	6.4	7.3	4.9	8.2	13.4

Source: Keesing's (1997: 41698)

Ireland: Seats

	1979	1984	1989	1994
Fianna Fáil	5	8	6	7
Fine Gael	4	6	4	4
Labour	4	—	1	1
Greens	—	—	—	2
Independent	2	1	2	1
Progressive Democrats	—	—	1	—
Democratic Left	—	—	1	—

Italy: Votes

Party	EP group	European election results				National elections	
		1979	1984	1989	1994	1994	1996
		%	%	%	%	%	%
Forza Italia	FE	—	—	—	30.6 }		20.6
Northern League	ELDRNA	—	—	1.8	6.6 }	}42.9	10.1
National Alliance (formerly MSI)	NA	5.4	6.5	5.5	12.5 }		15.7
Party of Democratic Left (PDS)	PES	29.6	33.3	27.6	19.1 }	}32.2	21.1
Refounded Communists	EU/NGL	—	—	—	6.1 }		8.6
Italian Popular Party (ex-CDs)	EPP	36.4	33.0	32.9	10.0 }	}15.7	6.8
Segni List (ex-CDs)	EPP	—	—	—	3.3 }		
Radicals, Liberals & Republicans	ELDR/ERA	9.9	9.5	4.4	3.0		
Greens	Green	—	—	6.2	3.2		
Socialist Party (PSI-AD)	PES	11.0	11.2	14.8	1.8		
Social Democratic Party (PSDI)	NA	4.3	3.5	2.7	0.7		
Others	EPP/Green	3.4	3.0	4.1	3.1	9.2	17.3

Source: Keesing's (1996: 41054)

Italy: Seats

	1979	1984	1989	1994
Forza Italia	—	—	—	27
Northern League	—	—	2	6
National Alliance (formerly MSI)	4	5	4	11
Party of Democratic Left (PDS)	24	27	22	16
Refounded Communists	—	—	—	5
Italian Popular Party (ex-CDs)	29	26	26	8
Segni List (ex-CDs)	—	—	0	3
Radicals, Liberals & Republicans	8	8	4	3
Greens	—	—	5	3
Socialist Party (PSI-AD)	9	9	12	2
Social Democratic Party (PSDI)	4	3	2	1
Others	3	3	4	2

Luxembourg: Votes

Party	EP group	European election results				National elections
		1979 %	1984 %	1989 %	1994 %	1994 %
Christian Social People's Party (CSV)	EPP	36.1	34.9	34.9	31.4	29.5
Socialist Workers' Party (LSAP)	PES	21.7	29.9	25.4	24.8	30.4
Democratic Party (DP)	ELDR	28.1	22.1	20.0	18.9	14.5
Green List	Green	—	6.1	10.4	10.9	10.1
Communists (KPL)		5.0	4.1	4.7	—	2.4
ADR (formerly 5/6 Action Committee)		—	—	—	—	7.7
Others		9.1	2.9	4.6	14.0	5.4

Source: Hearl (1994)

Luxembourg: Seats

	1979	1984	1989	1994
Christian Social People's Party (CSV)	3	3	3	2
Socialist Workers' Party (LSAP)	1	2	2	2
Democratic Party (DP)	2	1	1	1
Green List	—	—	—	1
Communists (KPL)	—	—	—	—
Others	—	—	—	—

The Netherlands: Votes

Party	EP group	European election results				National elections	
		1979 %	1984 %	1989 %	1994 %	1994 %	1998 %
Christian Democrats (CDA)	EPP	35.6	30.0	34.6	30.8	22.2	18.4
Labour Party (PvdA)	PES	30.4	33.7	30.7	22.9	24.0	29.0
Freedom & Democracy Party (VVD)	ELDR	16.2	18.9	13.6	17.9	19.9	24.7
Democrats 66 (D'66)	ELDR	9.0	2.3	5.9	11.7	15.5	9.0
Greens (Rainbow in 1984 & 1989)	Green	—	5.6	7.0	6.1	3.5	7.3
Coalition of Orthodox Protestants	I-EN	—	5.2	5.9	7.8	4.8	—
Others		8.8	4.3	2.3	2.8	10.1	11.6

Sources: Royal Netherlands Embassy, London; Keesing's (1998: 42293)

The Netherlands: Seats

	1979	1984	1989	1994
Christian Democrats (CDA)	10	8	10	10
Labour Party (PvdA)	9	9	8	8
Freedom & Democracy Party (VVD)	4	5	3	6
Democrats 66 (D'66)	2	—	1	4
Greens (Rainbow in 1984 & 1989)	—	2	2	1
Coalition of Orthodox Protestants	—	1	1	2
Others	—	—	—	—

Portugal: Votes

Party	EP Group	European election results			National
		1987	1989	1994	1995
		%	%	%	%
Social Democratic Party (PSD)	ELDR*	38.4	32.7	34.4	34.0
Socialist Party (PS)	PES	23.1	28.5	34.8	43.9
United Democratic Alliance (CDU)	EUL/NGL	11.8	14.4	11.2	8.9
Social Democratic Centre (CDS)	UFE	15.8	14.1	12.5	9.1
Others (incl. invalid papers)		10.9	10.3	7.1	4.1

Source: Portuguese Embassy, London.
* MEPS joined the EPP Group in 1996.

Portugal: Seats

	1987	1989	1994
Social Democratic Party (PSD)	10	9	9
Socialist Party (PS)	6	8	10
United Democratic Alliance (CDU)	3	4	3
Social Democratic Centre (CDS)	4	3	3
Others (incl. invalid papers)	1	—	—

Spain: Votes

Party	EP group	European election results			National elections	
		1987 %	1989 %	1994 %	1993 %	1996 %
Socialist Workers' Party (PSOE)	PES	39.1	40.2	30.7	38.6	37.5
Popular Party (PP)	EPP	24.7	21.7	40.2	34.8	38.9
United Left (IU)	EUL/NGL	5.2	6.2	13.5	9.5	10.6
Catalan Party	EPP/ELDR	4.4	4.3	4.7	5.0	4.6
Democrat & Social Centre		10.3	7.2	1.0	—	—
Nationalist Coalition (regional parties)	EPP/ERA	—	1.9	2.8	—	—
European People's Coalition		1.7	1.5	1.3	—	—
Andalucian Party		1.0	1.9	0.8	—	—
Regional Left Party		1.3	1.9	—	—	—
Basque Party (Herri Batasuna)		1.9	1.7	1.0	0.8	—
Supporters of Ruiz Mateos		—	3.9	—	—	—
Galicia National Party		—	—	0.8	—	—
Greens		—	—	0.7	—	—
Others		10.4	7.8	2.4	11.4	8.4

Source: Keesing's (1996: 41008)

Spain: Seats

	1987	1989	1994
Socialist Workers' Party (PSOE)	28	27	22
Popular Party (PP)	17	15	28
United Left (IU)	3	4	9
Catalan Party	3	2	3
Democrat & Social Centre	7	5	—
Nationalist Coalition (regional parties)	—	1	2
European People's Coalition	1	1	—
Andalucian Party	—	1	—
Regional Left Party	—	1	—
Basque Party (Herri Batasuna)	1	1	—
Supporters of Ruiz Mateos	—	2	—
Galicia National Party	—	—	—
Greens	—	—	—

United Kingdom: Votes

Party	EP group	European election results				National elections	
		1979 %	1984 %	1989 %	1994 %	1992 %	1997 %
Labour	PES	31.6	36.5	40.1	42.7	34.4	43.2
Conservatives	EPP	48.4	40.8	34.1	26.8	41.9	30.7
Scottish National Party (SNP)	ERA	1.9	1.7	2.7	3.1	1.9	2.0
Liberal Democrats	ELDR	12.6	19.5	6.4	16.1	17.8	16.8
Greens		—	0.6	15.0	3.1	—	—
Plaid Cymru		0.6	0.7	0.8	1.0	0.5	0.5
Democratic Ulster Unionists (DUP)	NA	1.3	1.6	1.0	1.0 }		
Social Democratic & Labour Party (SDLP)	PES	1.1	1.1	0.9	1.0	} 2.2	0.6
Official Ulster Unionist Party (OUP)	EPP	0.9	1.1	0.8	0.8 }		
Others		1.6	0.9	1.5	4.4	1.3	—

Source: Keesing's (1997: 41647)

United Kingdom: Seats

	1979	1984	1989	1994
Labour	17	32	45	62
Conservatives	60	45	32	18
Scottish National Party (SNP)	1	1	1	2
Liberal Democrats	—	—	—	2
Greens	—	—	—	—
Plaid Cymru	—	—	—	—
Democratic Ulster Unionists (DUP)	1	1	1	1
Social Democratic & Labour Party (SDLP)	1	1	1	1
Official Ulster Unionist Party (OUP)	1	1	1	1

Austrian Election Results

Party	EP group	European election (1996)		National (1995)
		Votes %	Seats	%
Austrian People's Party (ÖVP)	EPP	29.6	7	28.3
Social Democratic Party of Austria (SPÖ)	PES	29.1	6	38.1
Freedom Party of Austria (FPÖ)	NA	27.6	6	21.9
Greens	Greens	6.7	1	4.8
Liberal Forum	ELDR	4.2	1	5.5
Others		0.8	—	1.4
Turnout		67.21%		82.70%

Sources: Keesing's (1996: 41334; 1995: 40877)

Finnish Election Results

Party	EP group	European election (1996)		National (1995)
		Votes %	Seats	%
		%		
Centre Party (KESK)	ELDR	24.4	4	19.9
Finnish Social Democratic Party (SDP)	PES	21.5	4	28.3
National Coalition Party (KOK)	EPP	20.2	4	17.9
Left-Wing Alliance (VL)	EUL/NGL	10.5	2	11.2
Green League	Greens	7.6	1	6.5
Swedish People's Party (SFP)	ELDR	5.7	1	5.1
Others		10.1	—	12.1
Turnout		58.8%		68.6%

Sources: Keesing's (1996: 41333-4; 1995:40468)

Swedish Election Results

Party	EP group	European election (1995)		National (1998)
		Votes %	Seats	%
Social Democratic Labour Party (SAP)	PES	28.1	7	36.6
Moderate Unity Party (M)	EPP	23.1	5	22.7
Left Party (Vp)	EUL/NGL	12.9	3	12.0
Christian Democrats (KD)		—	—	11.8
Centre Party (C)	ELDR	7.2	2	5.1
Liberal Party (FpL)	ELDR	4.8	1	4.7
Green Party (MpG)	Greens	17.2	4	4.5
Others		6.7		2.6
Turnout		41.3%		81.4%

Sources: Keesing's (1998: 42515; 1995: 40743)

Bibliography

NB. The following abbreviations relate to archival material located in the European Communities Archives, European University Institute in Florence

ME   International European Movement Papers
PE2   Minutes and Reports of the Ad Hoc Assembly
PU   Pierre Uri Papers

Act concerning the election of the representatives of the European Parliament by direct universal suffrage, 1976.
Ad Hoc Assembly
    1952a   *Assemblée commune bureau: Rapport sur les travaux de la commission constitutionelle de l'assemblée 'Ad Hoc' 15 septembre–15 octobre*, PE2/42.
    1952b   Constitutional Committee of the Ad Hoc Assembly—Second Session—*Minutes of the First Meeting Held on 23 October 1952*, PE2/24.
    1952c   *Compte-rendu analytique de la 2ème séance tenue le 24 octobre 1952*, PE2/26.
    1952d   *Verbatim Report of the Proceedings of 25 October 1952*, PE2/26.
    1952e   *Verbatim Report of the Proceedings of the First Session Held on 15 December 1952*, PE2/26.
    1952f   *Compte-rendu de la 3ème séance tenue le 17 décembre 1952*, PE2/26.
    1952g   *Verbatim Report of the Proceedings of 18 December 1952*, PE2/27.
    1952h   *Questions relatives à la création d'une Communauté Politique Européenne*, PE2/21.
    1952i   *Exposé des motifs* of the Working Group, PE2/28.
Aldrich, Richard J.
    1995   'European Integration: An American Intelligence Connection', in Anne Deighton (ed.), *Building Postwar Europe: National Decision-makers and European Institutions, 1948–63* (Basingstoke: Macmillan in association with St Antony's College, Oxford): 159-79.
Almond, Gabriel A., and Sidney Verba
    1989   *The Civic Culture: Political Attitudes and Democracy in Five Nations* (London: Sage Publications).
American Institute for Contemporary German Studies
    1999   http://www.jhu.edu/~aicgsdoc?wahlen/elect98.htm#stats.

Anastassopoulos, Georgios
    1998   'Report on a proposal for an electoral procedure incorporating common principles for the election of Members of the European Parliament'.
Archibugi, Daniele, and David Held (eds.)
    1995   *Cosmopolitan Democracy: An Agenda for a New World Order* (Cambridge: Polity Press).
Archibugi, Daniele, David Held and Martin Köhler (eds.)
    1998   *Re-imagining Political Community* (Cambridge: Polity Press).
Anglo-French discussions regarding French proposals for the Western European coal, iron and steel industries, *Mission Hirsch/Uri à Londres, 5/50*, Document 2, PU/20.
Bagehot, Walter
    1963   *The English Constitution* (intro. R.H.S. Crossman; London: Collins, 1963).
Bangemann, Martin
    1978   'Preparations for Direct Elections in the Federal Republic of Germany', *Common Market Law Review* 15: 321-38.
Bardi, Luciano
    1996   'Transnational Trends in European Parties and the 1994 Elections of the European Parliament', *Party Politics* 2.1: 99-114.
Barton, Roger
    1995   'Report on the Joint Text of the Conciliation Committee for a European Parliament and Council Directive on the Maximum Design Speed, Maximum Torque and Maximum Net Engine Power of Two or Three Wheel Motor Vehicles (C4-0010/95—0371[COD])' (Brussels: European Parliament: 17 January 1995).
Beesley, Hugh
    1963   'Direct Elections to the European Parliament', in *Limits and Problems of European Integration: The Conference of May 30–June 2 1961* (intro. B. Landheer; The Hague: Martinus Nijhoff).
Beetham, David
    1991   *The Legitimation of Power* (London: Macmillan).
Beetham, David, and Christopher Lord
    1998   *Legitimacy and the European Union* (London: Longman).
Benvenuti Report
    1952   'Report on the Powers and Competence of European Political Community Submitted on Behalf of the Sub-Committee on Powers and Competence by M. Benvenuti, Rapporteur', 3rd Session of the Ad Hoc Assembly's Constitutional Committee, 13 December, PE2/106.
Benvenuti *et al.*
    1952   *Statut de la Communauté Européenne: Projet de rédaction présenté par Benvenuti, Dehousse et von Merkatz, Rapporteurs*, PE2/40.
Birch, Anthony H.
    1971   *Representation* (London: Pall Mall Press).
    1993   *The Concepts and Theories of Modern Democracy* (London: Routledge).
Blais, André, and R.K. Carty
    1990   'Does Proportional Representation Foster Voter Turnout?', *European Journal of Political Research* 18.2: 167-81.

1991 'The Psychological Impact of Electoral Laws: Measuring Duverger's Elusive Factor', *British Journal of Political Science* 21.1: 79-93.

Blondel, Jean, Richard Sinnott and Palle Svensson
1997 'Representation and Voter Participation', *European Journal of Political Research* 32.2: 243-72.

Bogdanor, Vernon
1986 'The Future of the European Community: Two Models of Democracy', *Government and Opposition* 21.2: 161-76.
1989a 'The June 1989 European Elections and the Institutions of the Community', *Government and Opposition* 24.2: 199-214.
1989b 'Direct Elections, Representative Democracy and European Integration', *Electoral Studies* 8.3: 205-16.
1990 *Democratizing the Community* (London: Federal Trust for Education and Research).

Bowles, Nigel
1993 *The Government and Politics of the United States* (London: Macmillan).

Bradley, Kieran St Clair
1994 Member of the Legal Secretariat of the European Parliament, Interview with the author, 30 November.

Brugmans, Henrik
1970 'Foreword' to Patijn (1970): 8-15.

Bryce, Lord
1921 'The Decline of Legislatures', in Lord Bryce, *Modern Democracies ii* (London: Macmillan):367-77, reprinted in Norton (ed.) 1990c: 47-56.

Butler, David, and Donald Stokes
1974 *Political Change in Britain: The Evolution of Electoral Choice* (London: Macmillan, 2nd edn).

Butler, David, and David Marquand
1981 *European Elections and British Politics* (London: Longman).

Butler, David, and Martin Westlake
1995 *British Politics and European Elections 1994* (London: Macmillan).

Camps, Miriam
1964 *Britain and the European Community 1955–1963* (London: Oxford University Press).
1966 *European Unification in the Sixties: From the Veto to the Crisis* (New York: McGraw-Hill).

Cardozo, Rita
1987 'The Project for a Political Community: 1952-54' in Pryce (ed.) 1987: 49-77.

Cardozo, Rita, and Richard Corbett
1985 'The Crocodile Initiative', in Juliet Lodge (ed.), *European Union: The European Community in Search of the Future* (London: Macmillan): 15-46.

Chryssochoou, Dimitris
1994 'Democracy and Symbiosis in the European Union: Towards a Confederal Consociation?', *West European Politics* 17.4: 1-14.
1998 *Democracy in the European Union* (London: Tauris Academic Studies).

Commission of the European Communities
  1969   *Memorandum to the Conference of Heads of State or Government in The Hague*, 19 November 1969, in *Bull EC* 1/1970.
Congress of Europe at The Hague
  1948a   *Verbatim Report of the Proceedings of the Political Committee, 8 May*, ME/392.
  1948b   *Verbatim Report of the Proceedings, 9 May*, ME/393.
  1948c   *Draft of Final Resolution of Political Committee*, ME/440.
  1948d   *Minutes and Resolutions of the Congress, 7 May*, ME/421.
  1948e   *Preliminary Draft Resolution for the Political Report*, ME/1182.
  1948f   *Resolutions of the Congress*, ME/1122.
Corbett, Richard
  1989   'Testing the New Procedures: The European Parliament's First Experiences with its New "Single Act" Powers', *Journal of Common Market Studies* 27.4: 359-72.
  1998   *The European Parliament's Role in Closer EC Integration* (London: Macmillan).
Corbett, Richard, Francis Jacobs and Michael Shackleton
  1995   *The European Parliament* (London: Cartermill, 3rd edn).
Coudenhove-Kalergi, Count Richard
  1948   Speech to the Congress of the Hague, Session plenière d'ouverture du vendredi 7 mai 1948.
Curtice, John
  1989   'The 1989 European Election: Protest or Green Tide?', *Electoral Studies* 8.3: 217-30.
Dahl, Robert A.
  1994   'A Democratic Dilemma: System Effectiveness versus Citizen Participation', *Political Science Quarterly* 109.1: 23-34.
Dalton, Russell J.
  1988   *Citizen Politics in Western Democracies: Public Opinion and Political Parties in the United States, Great Britain, West Germany and France* (Chatham, NJ: Chatham House Publishers, Inc.).
Debré, Michel
  1953   *Proposition de résolution tendant à établir un pacte pour une union d'états européens*, January 1953, PE2/37.
De Gucht Report
  1993   *European Parliament Resolution* A3-0381/92.
Dehousse Report
  1960   Report reprinted in *Pour l'élection de PEG au suffrage universel direct*, (PEG: Luxembourg, 1969), includes the Faure Report on the 'Composition of the Elected Parliament' and the Schuijt Report on 'Questions Relating to the Electoral System of the Parliament to be Elected'.
Deth, Jan W. van
  1991   'Politicization and Political Interest' in Reif and Inglehart (eds.) 1991: 201-13.

Deutsch, Karl W.
  1953   *Nationalism and Social Communication: An Inquiry into the Foundations of Nationality* (London: Chapman and Hall).
  1954   *Political Community at the International Level* (New York: Doubleday).
  1968   *The Analysis of International Relations* (Englewood Cliffs, NJ: Prentice–Hall).
Deutsch, Karl W., Lewis J. Edinger, Roy C. Macridis and Richard L. Merritt
  1967   *France, Germany and the Western Alliance: A Study of Elite Attitudes on European Integration and World Politics* (New York: Charles Scribner's Sons).
Deutsch, Karl W., and William J. Foltz (eds.)
  1963   *Nation-Building* (London: Prentice–Hall).
Draft Convention on the Election of Members of the European Parliament by Direct Universal Suffrage, 1975, in *Bull EC* 1/1975.
Duchêne, François
  1994   *Jean Monnet: The First Statesman of Interdependence* (London: W.W. Norton).
Duff, Andrew
  1994   'Building a Parliamentary Europe', *Government and Opposition* 29.2: 147-65.
Duff, Andrew (ed.)
  1997   *The Treaty of Amsterdam: Text and Commentary* (London: Federal Trust).
Dunn, John (ed.)
  1992   *Democracy: The Unfinished Journey 508 BC to AD 1993* (Oxford: Oxford University Press).
Duverger, Maurice
  1954   *Political Parties* (London: Methuen).
Eijk, Cees van der, Mark Franklin and Michael Marsh
  1996   'What Can Voters Teach Us about Europe-wide Elections? What Can Europe-wide Elections Teach Us about Voters?', *Electoral Studies* 15.2: 149-66.
ELDR
  1995   *Short History of the European Liberal, Democrat and Reform Party* (Brussels: The European Liberal, Democrat and Reform Party, 4th edn).
Eurobarometer Trends 1974–94
Eurobarometer 41 Spring 1994
European Coal and Steel Community
  1951   *Note générale sur la communauté européenne du Charbon et de l'Acier*, August 1951, PU/32.
European Movement
  1949   *Europe Unites: The Hague Congress and After* (London: Hollis and Carter).
European Parliament
  1969   *Pour l'élection de PEG au suffrage universel direct* (Luxembourg: PEG).
  1992a   *40th Anniversary Proceedings of the Symposium: The European Community in the Historical Context of its Parliament* (Strasbourg: European Parliament).

European Parliament

1992b   *Documents on Political Union* (Dublin: European Parliament).

1992c   *Resolution A3-0123/92 of the European Parliament, the Resolution on the Intergovernmental Conferences.*

1993   *Minutes of the sitting of Wednesday, 15 September 1993* (PE 174.510).

1994a   *Election Special June 1994, The Outgoing Parliament/1989–1994/The Candidates* (Brussels: European Parliament, Doc EN\DV\252\252337).

1994b   *Info Memo 'Special Elections': XVIII Session Constitutive Le Nouveau PE au 19 Juillet 1994* (Brussels: EP, Directorate of the Press).

1994c   *Results and Elected Members* (Brussels: European Parliament), Provisional Edition 15 June.

1994d   *Info Memo 'Election Special' No.1* (Brussels: European Parliament Directorate General for Information and Public Relations).

1994e   *Report on the Budgetary Procedure: 1994 Financial Year* (Brussels: European Parliament, Doc_EN\DV\248\248034).

1994f   Memorandum to the Members of the Committee on the Budgets (Brussels: EP, Doc_EN\DV\251\251401, 1 July 1994).

1995a   *Info Memo 1* (Brussels: EP Directorate General of the Press, 4 January).

1995b   *Info Memo Special No. 8*, Hearings of European Commissioners-Designate from Wednesday, 4 January to Tuesday, 10 January 1995 (Brussels: EP Directorate General of the Press).

1995c   *Strasbourg Notebook* (European Parliament, Directorate-General for Information and Public Relations, 18 January).

1995d   *Les Commissions Spécialisées dans les Affaires Européennes des Parlements des Etats Membres* (Brussels: EP, Direction Général des Commissions et Délégations [Division pour les rélations avec les Parlements des Etats membres] En collaboration avec la Direction Général des Etudes [Centre Européen de Recherche et de Documentation Parlementaire], draft of May 1995).

1996   'Background Information, 21-10-1996'. Internet site: www.europarl.eu.int/dg3/sdp/backg/en/1996/b961021.htm.

1998a   *Rules of Procedure* (Luxembourg: European Parliament, 13th edn).

1998b   *News Report 09-12-98* (Brussels: European Parliament, web version: http://www.europarl.eu.int/dg3/sdp/newsrp/en/n981209.htm).

1998c   *The Specialised Committees on European Affairs in the Parliaments of the Member States and Applicant Countries* (Brussels: European Parliament Directorate-General for Committees and Delegations, Division 'Relations with national parliaments and interparliamentary Assemblies').

1998d   *Info Session, Avant-Première Session Parlementaire Bruxelles, 2-3 décembre* (Brussels: European Parliament).

1998e   *News Report: 10-12-98* (Brussels: European Parliament, web version: http://www.europarl.eu.int/dg3/sdp/newsrp/en/n981210.htm).

1999a   *Background information: 06-01-99* (Brussels: European Parliament, web version: http://www.europarl.eu.int/dg3/sdp/backg/en/b990106.htm)

1999b   *Briefing: 11-01-99* (Brussels: European Parliament, web version: http://www.europarl.eu.int/dg3/sdp/brief/en/b990111s.htm).

1999c   'Political Groups in the European Parliament as at 27.01.99', PE 275.729.

1999d   'Resolution on Improving the Financial Management of the Commis-
             sion', 14 January; http://www.europarl.eu.int
Faure Report
1960   Report on the 'Composition of the Elected Parliament', repr. in European
             Parliament 1969.
Featherstone, Kevin
1986   'Greece' in Lodge (ed.) 1986: 117-37.
1994   'Jean Monnet and the "Democratic Deficit" in the European Union',
             Journal of Common Market Studies 32.2: 149-70.
Fitzmaurice, John
1978   *The European Parliament* (Hampshire: Gower).
1988   'An Analysis of the European Community's Co-operation Procedure',
             Journal of Common Market Studies 26.4: 389-400.
Foltz, William J.
1963   'Building the Newest Nations: Short-run Strategies and Long-run
             Problems' in Deutsch and Foltz (eds.) 1963.
Franklin, Mark N., and Thomas T. Mackie
1991   'The Use of Eurobarometer Data in the Study of Electoral Change' in
             Reif and Inglehart (eds.) 1991: 244-55.
Furler Report
1963   'Report on the Competences and Powers of the European Parliament', in
             Parlement Européen, *Documents de Séance 1963–64*, Doc 31, 14 June.
Fursdon, Major-General Edward
1980   *The European Defence Community: A History* (London: Macmillan).
Gaffney, John (ed.)
1996   *Political Parties and the European Union* (London: Routledge).
George, Stephen
1989   *Nationalism, Liberalism and the National Interest: Britain, France and
             the European Community* (Strathclyde Papers on Government and
             Politics, No. 67; Department of Politics, University of Strathclyde).
Gerbet, Pierre
1987   'In Search of Political Union: The Fouchet Plan negotiations', in Pryce
             (ed.) 1987: 105-29.
1992   'The Common Assembly of the European Coal and Steel Community', in
             European Parliament (1992a): 11-16.
Haas, Ernst
1958   *The Uniting of Europe: Political, Social and Economic Forces* (London:
             Stevens and Sons).
Haas, Ernst B., and Allen S. Whiting
1956   *Dynamics of International Relations* (New York: McGraw-Hill).
Haigh, Nigel, and David Baldock
1989   *Environmental Policy and 1992* (a report prepared for the British
             Department of the Environment on the consequences for environmental
             policy of the completion of the EC internal market; London: HMSO).
Hallstein, Walter
1951   *Der Schuman Plan von Dr. iur. Walter Hallstein*, Speech on 28 April
             1951 (Frankfurt am Main: Vittorio Klostermann).

Hallstein, Walter
    1962   *United Europe: Challenge and Opportunity* (London: Oxford University
                Press).
    1972   *Europe in the Making* (London: George Allen & Unwin).
Harper, John L.
    1996   'In their Own Image: The Americans and the Question of European
                Unity, 1943-1954', in Martyn Bond, Julie Smith and William Wallace,
                (eds.), *Eminent Europeans* (London: Greycoat Press): 62-84.
Hayward, Fred M.
    1971   'Continuities and Discontinuities between Studies of National and
                International Political Integration: Some Implications for Future Research
                Efforts', in Lindberg and Scheingold (eds.) 1971: 313-37.
Heads of State or Government
    1970   'Communiqué', in *Bull EC* 1/1970.
Heads of Government
    1974   'Communiqué of the Conference of Heads of Government in Paris' (9
                and 10 December 1974), in *Bull EC* 12/1974.
Hearl, D.
    1994   'Notes on the Elections to the European Parliament', *Electoral Studies*
                13.4: 331-67.
Heath, Anthony, Roger Jowell, John Curtice and Bridget Taylor
    1995   *The 1994 European and Local Elections: Abstention, Protest and
                Conversion* (Paper presented at the Political Studies Association Annual
                Conference at the University of York, 18-20 April 1995).
Held, David (ed.)
    1991a   *Political Theory Today* (Cambridge: Polity Press)
Held, David
    1991b   'Democracy, the Nation-State and the Global System', in Held (1991a):
                197-235.
    1992   'Democracy: From City-states to a Cosmopolitan Order?', *Political
                Studies* Special Issue 40: 10-39.
    1995   *Democracy and the Global Order: From the Modern State to
                Cosmopolitan Order* (Cambridge: Polity Press).
Henig, Stanley (ed.)
    1979   *Political Parties in the European Community* (London: Allen & Unwin).
Herman, Valentine, and Juliet Lodge
    1978   *The European Parliament and the European Community* (London:
                Macmillan).
Hewstone, Miles
    1986   *Understanding Attitudes to the European Community: A Social-
                psychological Study in Four Member-states* (Cambridge: Cambridge
                University Press).
Hix, Simon
    1993   'The Emerging EC Party System? The European Party Federations in the
                Intergovernmental Conferences', *Politics* 13.2: 38-46.
    1994   *A History of the Party of European Socialists* (Research Series No. 1;
                Brussels: European Parliament).
    1996   'The Transnational Party Federations', in Gaffney (ed.) 1996: 308-31.

Hix, Simon, and Christopher Lord
    1996   'The Making of a President: The European Parliament and the Confirmation of Jacques Santer as President of the Commission', *Government and Opposition* 31: 62-76.
    1997   *Political Parties in the European Union* (London: Macmillan).

Hofricher, Jürgen, and Michael Klein
    1993   *The European Parliament in the Eyes of EC Citizens* (Report on behalf of the European Parliament, Directorate General III, Information and Public Relations).

Hogan, Michael J.
    1987   *The Marshall Plan: America, Britain and the Reconstruction of Western Europe, 1947–1952* (Cambridge: Cambridge University Press).

Hogan, Willard N.
    1967   *Representation, Government and European Integration* (Lincoln: University of Nebraska Press).

Institute for Democracy and Electoral Studies
    1999   Internet site: www.idea.int/voter_turnout/westeurope/index.htlm.

Ionescu, Ghita
    1971   'The New Politics of European Integration', *Government and Opposition* Special Issue 1971: 417-21.

Irwin, Galen
    1995   'Second-order or Third-rate? Issues in the Campaign for the European Parliament 1994', *Electoral Studies* 14.2, 183-99.

Jackman, Robert W.
    1987   'Political Institutions and Voter Turnout in the Industrial Democracies', *American Political Science Review* 81.2: 405-23.

Jackson, Caroline
    1993   'The First British MEPs', *Contemporary European History* 2.2: 169-95.

Jackson, Robert, and John Fitzmaurice
    1979   *The European Parliament: A Guide to Direct Elections* (Harmondsworth: Penguin Books).

Jacobs, Francis, Richard Corbett and Michael Shackleton
    1992   *The European Parliament* (Harlow: Longman, 2nd edn)

Jansen, Thomas
    1998   *The European People's Party: Origins and Developments* (London: Macmillan).

Janssens Report
    1963   *Document de travail sur l'évolution des institutions communautaires et leur coopération en rapport avec les responsabilités croissantes de la Communauté* (Doc 101/1962-1963).

Keesing's
    1995   *Record of World Events*
    1996   *Record of World Events*
    1997   *Record of World Events*
    1998   *Record of World Events*

Ketteler, Thomas, Dietrich Rometsch and Wolfgang Wessels
    1993   *Survey: Academic Works and Studies on the European Parliament: Stocktaking of the 'State of the Art' and the 'Acquis Académique':*

Agenda Setting for Major Desiderata in Research and Training (Bonn: Institut für Europäische Politik).

King, Anthony
    1968   'Why all Governments Lose By-elections', *New Society* 21 March 1968: 413-15.
Klepsch, Dr Egon
    1992   'Address to the symposium to mark the 40th Anniversary of the European Parliament in 1992' in European Parliament (1992a): 5-10.
Küsters, Hans Jürgen
    1989   'Jean Monnet and the European Union: idea and reality of the integration process', in Giandomenico Majone, Emile Noël and Peter van der Bossche (eds.), *Jean Monnet et l'Europe d'aujourd'hui* (Baden-Baden: Nomos Verlagsgesellschaft).
Lakeman, Enid
    1991   *Twelve Democracies: Electoral Systems in the European Community* (London: The Arthur McDougall Fund).
Lindberg, Leon N.
    1963   *The Political Dynamics of European Economic Integration* (London: Oxford University Press).
Lindberg, Leon N., and Stuart A. Scheingold
    1970   *Europe's Would-be Polity: Patterns of Change in the European Community* (Englewood Cliffs, NJ: Prentice-Hall).
Lindberg, Leon N., and Stuart A. Scheingold (eds.)
    1971   *Regional Integration: Theory and Research* (Cambridge, MA: Harvard University Press).
Lipset, Seymour Martin, and Stein Rokkan (eds.)
    1967   *Party Systems and Voter Alignments: Cross-national Perspectives* (New York: The Free Press) Introduction: 1-64 (repr. Peter Mair [ed.], *The West European Party System* [Oxford: Oxford University Press, 1990]: 91-138).
Llobera, Josep R.
    1993   'The Role of the State and the Nation in Europe', in Soledad García (ed.), *European Identity and the Search for Legitimacy* (London: Pinter): 64-80.
Lodge, Juliet
    1984   'The 1984 Euro-elections: A Damp Squib?', *The World Today*, August–September 1984: 333-40.
    1990   *The 1989 Election of the European Parliament* (London: Macmillan).
Lodge, Juliet (ed.)
    1986   *Direct Elections to the European Parliament 1984* (London: Macmillan).
Lodge, Juliet, and Valentine Herman
    1980   'Direct Elections to the European Parliament: A Supranational Perspective', *European Journal of Political Research* 8.1: 45-62.
    1982   *Direct Elections to the European Parliament: A Community Perspective* (London: Macmillan).
Loewenberg, Gerhard (ed.)
    1971a   *Modern Parliaments: Change or Decline* (New York: Aldine Atherton).

Loewenberg, Gerhard (ed.)
    1971b   'The Role of Parliaments in Modern Political Systems' in Loewenberg
              (ed.) 1971a: 1-20.

Lord, Christopher
    1998   *Democracy in the European Union* (Contemporary European Studies, 4;
             Sheffield: Sheffield Academic Press).

Louis, Jean-Victor
    1992   'The European Parliament from 1958 to 1979', in European Parliament
             (1992a): 17-22.

Ludwig, Klemens
    1993   *Europa zerfällt: Volker ohne Staaten und der neue Nationalismus*
             (Hamburg: Rowohlt Taschenbuch Verlag GmbH).

Luxembourg Delegation to the Schuman Plan
    1950   *Projet de l'exposé des motifs de la loi portant approbation du Traité*
             instituant la Communauté Européenne du Charbon et de l'Acier (Version
             provisoire et incomplète), PU/35.

Mackay, R.W.G., MP
    1951   *European Unity: The Strasbourg Plan for a European Political Authority*
             with Limited Functions but Real Powers (Oxford: Basil Blackwell).

Mackenzie, W.J.M.
    1968   'The Functions of Elections' in David L. Sills (ed.), *International
             Encyclopedia of the Social Sciences* (London: Collier-Macmillan): 1-6.

Mackie, T.T.
    1990   *Europe Votes 3: European Parliamentary Elections 1989* (Dartmouth
             Publishing Company Ltd).

Marquand, David
    1979   *Parliament for Europe* (London: Jonathan Cape).

Marsh, David
    1994   *Germany after the Elections: What Now for Europe?* (RIIA Briefing
             Paper No. 12; London: Royal Institute of International Affairs).

Marsh, Michael, and Pippa Norris
    1997   'Political Representation in the European Parliament', *European Journal
             of Political Research* 32.2: 153-64.

Martin Report
    1995   Report on the functioning of the Treaty on European Union with a view
             to the 1996 Intergovernmental Conference—Implementation and devel-
             opment of the Union, 4 May (European Parliament Document PE
             212.450).

Maurer, Andreas
    1998   European Parliament Research Project No. IV/98/13, *(Co-) Governing
             after Maastricht: The European Parliament's Institutional performance
             1994–1998. Lessons for the implementation of the Treaty of Amsterdam*
             (Bonn: Institut für Europäische Politik).

McLean, Iain
    1987   *Public Choice: An Introduction* (Oxford: Basil Blackwell).
    1991   'Forms of Representation and Systems of Voting' in Held (ed.) 1991a:
             172-96.

Memorandum sur les Institutions, annexe to rapport sur les travaux poursuivis à Paris par les délégations des six pays du 20/6 au 10/8/50, PU:27b.

Merritt, Richard L.
1963   'Nation-Building in America: The Colonial Years', in Deutsch and Foltz (eds.) 1963.

Mezey, Michael
1979   'Classifying Legislatures', in Michael Mazey, *Comparative Legislatures* (Durham, NC: Duke University Press): 21-44; repr. in Norton (1990c): 149-76.

Michalski, Anna, and Helen Wallace
1992   *The European Community: The Challenge of Enlargement* (London: Royal Institute of International Affairs, 2nd edn).

Mill, J. S.
1993   'Considerations on Representative Government', in G. Williams (ed.), *Utilitarianism, Liberty, and Representative Government* (London: J.M. Dent).

Miller, W. L., and M. Mackie
1975   'The Electoral Cycle and the Asymmetry of Government and Opposition Popularity: An Alternative Model of the Relationship between Economic Conditions and Political Popularity', *Political Studies* 21.3: 263-79.

Milward, Alan S.
1992   *The European Rescue of the Nation State* (London: Routledge).

Monnet, Jean
1951   *Audition de J. Monnet, M. Lagrange et P.Uri devant le Conseil de la République (10-11/7/1951)*, PU/37/3, 19 July.
1952   *Lettre à Pierre Pflimlin, 12 February 1951*, PU/40/4).
1972   Speech to the Friedrich Ebert Stiftung, 'L'Europe unie: de l'utopie à la réalité' (Lausanne: Centre de Recherches Européennes).

Morgan, Roger, and Clare Tame (eds.)
1996   *Parliaments and Parties: The European Parliament in the Political Life of Europe* (London: Macmillan).

Niedermayer, Oskar
1990   'Turnout in the European Elections', *Electoral Studies* 9.1: 45-50.
1991a   'The 1989 European Elections: Campaigns and Results', *European Journal of Political Research* 19: 3-16.
1991b   'Public Opinion about the European Parliament', in Reif and Inglehart (eds.) 1991: 27-44.

Norton, Philip
1987   'The House of Commons', in *The Blackwell Encyclopaedia of Political Institutions* (Oxford: Basil Blackwell): 273.
1990a   'Parliaments: A Framework for Analysis', *West European Politics*, Special Issue on 'Parliaments in Western Europe' 13.3: 1-9.
1990b   'Conclusion: Legislatures in Perspective', *West European Politics*, Special Issue on 'Parliaments in Western Europe' 13.3: 143-52.

Norton, Philip (ed.)
1990c   *Legislatures* (Oxford: Oxford University Press).
1996   *National Parliaments and the European Union* (London: Frank Cass).

Nye, Joseph S.
    1968   'Comparative Regional Integration: Concept and Measurement', *International Organization* 22.4: 855-80.

Oliver, Peter
    1996   'Electoral Rights under Article 8B of the Treaty of Rome', *Common Market Law Review* 33.3: 473-498.

Ollerenshaw, Steve
    1993   *The European Parliament: More Democracy or More Rhetoric? The European Parliament, the Single European Act, and the Interinstitutional Agreement* (Essex: Centre for European Studies, Occasional Papers in European Studies 2).

Oreja, Marcelino
    1994   Communication to Fernando Moran, 14 December.

Ortoli, François-Xavier
    1975   'Speech in the European Parliament's Debate on the Draft Convention on the Election of Members of the European Parliament by Direct Universal Suffrage', in *BullEC* 1/1975.

Packenham, Robert A.
    1970   'Legislatures and Political Development', in A. Kornberg and L.D. Musolf (eds.), *Legislatures in Developmental Perspective* (Durham NC: Duke University Press): 521-37, repr. in Norton (ed.) 1990c: 81-96.

Patijn Report
    1974   Adopted as European Parliament Resolution of 14 January 1975, Doc 368/74.

Patijn, Schelto (ed.)
    1970   *Landmarks in European Unity: 22 Texts on European Integration* (Leyden: A.W. Sijthoff).

Pentland, Charles
    1973   *International Theory and European Integration* (London: Faber and Faber).

Pinder, John
    1994   'The European Elections of 1994 and the Future of the European Union', *Government and Opposition* 29.1: 494-514.

Pflimlin, Pierre
    1950   *Communication du Ministre de l'Agriculture tendant à inviter le gouvernement à prendre l'initiative d'une organisation européenne des principaux marchés agricoles*, PU/40/3.

Pollack, Mark A.
    1994   'Creeping Competence: The Expanding Agenda of the European Community', *Journal of Public Policy* 14.2: 95-145.

Powell, G. Bingham Jr
    1980   'Voting Turnout in Thirty Democracies: Partisan, Legal and Socio-economic Influences', in Richard Rose (ed.), *Electoral Participation: A Comparative Analysis* (London: Sage Publications): 5-34.
    1986   'American Voter Turnout in Comparative Perspective', *American Political Science Review* 80.1: 17-43

Pridham, Geoffrey, and Pippa Pridham
 1979a 'The New European Party Federations and Direct Elections', *The World Today* 35: 62-70.
 1979b 'Transnational Parties in the European Community II: The Development of European Party Federations' in Henig (ed.) 1979: 278-98.
 1981 *Transnational Party Cooperation and European Integration: The Process towards Direct Elections* (London: Allen & Unwin).
Prout, Sir Christopher, QC, MEP
 1993 *The European Community and the 1994 European Elections* (The 1993 Alison Tennant Memorial Lecture, European Union of Women, 4th June 1993; London: Conservatives in the European Parliament).
Pryce, Roy (ed.)
 1987 *The Dynamics of European Union* (London: Croon Helm).
Rae, D. W.
 1967 *The Political Consequences of Electoral Laws* (New Haven, CN: Yale University Press).
Reif, Karlheinz (ed.)
 1984a *European Elections 1979/81 and 1984: Conclusions and Perspectives from Empirical Research* (Berlin: Quorum).
 1984b 'National Electoral Cycles and European Elections 1979 and 1984', *Electoral Studies* 3.3: 244-55.
 1985a *Ten European Elections: Campaigns and Results of the 1979/81 First Direct Elections to the European Parliament* (Aldershot: Gower).
Reif, Karlheinz, and Ronald Inglehart (eds.)
 1991 *Eurobarometer: The Dynamics of European Public Opinion. Essays in Honour of Jacques-René Rabier* (London: Macmillan).
Reif, Karlheinz, and Hermann Schmitt
 1980 'Nine Second-order National Elections: A Conceptual Framework for the Analysis of European Election Results', *European Journal of Political Research* 8.1: 3-44.
Research Services of the German Federal Parliament
 1993 'The Federal Constitutional Court's Maastricht Judgment (2 BvR 2134/92; 2 BvR 2159/92)', *Current Court Decisions No.9/93*, 22 October 1993.
Rey, Jean
 1970 '*Address to the European Parliament'*, 11 December 1969, in *Bull EC* 1/1970.
Reynaud, Paul
 1948 *Draft Resolution*, ME/440.
Roberts-Thomson, Patricia
 1998 'The "Crisis of Legitimacy" in the European Union and the EU Referendums'. Paper presented at the ECPR-ISA Joint Conference, Vienna, 16–19 September.
Rosas, Allan, and Esko Antola (eds.)
 1995 *A Citizens' Europe: In Search of a New Order* (London: Sage).
Rougemont, Denis de
 1948 *Preamble to the Congress of The Hague*, ME/388.

Sandys, Duncan
    1947   Memorandum by Chairman of Executive Committee on a 'Suggested Outline of Political Report for Congress of Europe', 21 December, ME/1182.

Sartori, Giovanni
    1968   'Democracy' in David L. Sills (ed.), *International Encylopedia of the Social Sciences* (London: Collier-Macmillan): 112-21.

Scheingold, Stuart A.
    1971   'Domestic and International Consequences of Regional Integration', in Lindberg and Scheingold (eds.) 1971: 374-98.

Schmuck, Otto
    1989   *Das Europäische Parlament: vom Gesprächsforum zum Mitgestalter europäische Politik* (Bonn).

Schöndube, Claus
    1992   'The European Parliament and Europe's Political Unity', in European Parliament 1992a: 33-8.

Schuijt Report
    1960   Report on 'Questions Relating to the Electoral System of the Parliament to Be Elected', repr. in European Parliament 1969.

Schulze, Hagen
    1992   'Nationalisme et identité nationale dans l'Europe des XIXe et XXe siècles', in Joseph Rovan and Gilbert Krebs (eds.), *Identités nationales et conscience européenne* (Publications de l'Institut d'Allemand d'Asnières).

Schuman Plan
    1950a   *Rapport des travaux poursuivis à Paris par les délégations des six pays du 20/6 au 10/8/50*, PU/27.
    1950b   *Document de travail élaboré par les experts français: juin 1950*, PU/26.
    1950c   *Résumé du document de travail présenté par les experts français: le 27 juin*, PU/26.
    1950d   *Modifications du document de travail français: juillet 1950*, PU/21.
    1950e   *Note générale sur le Plan Projet de traité et memorandum sur les dispositions transitoires état au 9/12/1950*, PU/31.

Shepherd, Robert J.
    1975   *Public Opinion and European Integration* (Farnborough: Saxon House).

Smith, Julie
    1994   *Citizens' Europe: The European Elections and the Role of the European Parliament* (London: Royal Institute of International Affairs).
    1995a   *Voice of the People: The European Parliament in the 1990s* (London: Royal Institute of International Affairs).
    1995b   'Appendix: The 1994 European Elections—Twelve into One Won't Go', *West European Politics*, Special Issue on 'The Crisis in Representation' 18.3: 199-217.
    1995c   'Direct Elections to the European Parliament: A Re-evaluation' (DPhil thesis, University of Oxford).
    1996   'How European are European Elections?' in Gaffney (ed.) 1996: 275-90.
    1997   *A Sense of Liberty: The History of the Liberal International 1947–97* (London: Liberal International).

Smith, M., L. Smith, and P.M.R. Stirk (eds.)
    1990   *Making the New Europe: European Unity and the Second World War*
        (London: Pinter).
Spaak Committee
    1955   *Document du travail No. 6 du Comité Intergouvernemental crée par la*
        conférence de Messine, 8 November 1955, PU153/5(A).
Spence, James
    1998   Head of Division, European Parliament Secretariat, Interview with the
        author, 3 December.
Spinelli, Altiero
    1984   *Introduction to the Draft Treaty Establishing the European Union*
        (Directorate-General for Information and Public Relations:Luxembourg).
Steed, Michael
    1971   'The European Parliament: The Significance of Direct Elections',
        Government and Opposition, Special Issue on 'The New Politics of
        European Integration' 6.4: 462-76.
Stevens, Chris
    1996   'EU Policy for the Banana Market' in Wallace and Wallace (eds.) 1996:
        325-51.
Stokes, Donald, and W.E. Miller
    1962   'Party Government and the Saliency of Congress', *Public Opinion*
        Quarterly 26.4: 531-46.
Taagepera, Rein, and Matthew S. Shugart
    1989   'Designing Electoral Systems', *Electoral Studies* 8.1: 49-58.
Thune, Christian
    1994   'Denmark' in Werner Weidenfeld and Wolfgang Wessels (eds.),
        Jahrbuch der Europäischen Integration 1993/94 (Bonn: Europa Union):
        313-18.
Tiilikainen, Teija
    1995   'The Problem of Democracy in the European Union' in Rosas and Antola
        (eds.) 1995: 19-38.
Tindemans Report
    1976   'European Union: Report to the European Council' in *Bull EC*
        Supplement 1/76.
Tindemans, Leo
    1994   Interview with the author, 16 November.
Tranholm-Mikkelsen, J.
    1991   'Neo-functionalism: Obstinate or Obsolete? A Reappraisal in the Light of
        the New Dynamism of the EC', *Millennium* 20.1: 1-22.
Tufte, Edward R.
    1975   'Determinants of the Outcomes of the Midterm Congressional Elections',
        American Political Science Review 69.4: 812-26.
Urwin, Derek
    1991   *The Community of Europe: A History of European Integration Since*
        1945 (London: Longman).
Vedel Report
    1972   'Report of the Working Party Examining the Problem of the Enlargement
        of the Powers of the European Parliament', in *Bull EC Supplement* 4/72.

Vedel, Georges
    1975   'Le rôle de l'institution parlementaire dans l'intégration européenne', Parlement européen. *L'intégration européenne et l'avenir du parlement en Europe*, Symposium in 1974 (Luxembourg: EP).

Vredeling, H.
    1971   'The Common Market of Political Parties', *Government and Opposition*, Special Issue on 'The New Politics of European Integration' 6.4: 448-61.

Wahlke, John C.
    1971   'Policy Demands and System Support: The Role of the Represented', *British Journal of Political Science* 1: 521-37; repr. in Norton (ed.) 1990c: 97-123.

Wallace, Helen
    1979a   'The European Parliament: The Challenge of Political Responsibility', *Government and Opposition* 14.4: 433-43.
    1979b   'Direct Elections and the Political Dynamics of the European Communities', *Journal of Common Market Studies* 17.4: 281-96.

Wallace, Helen, and William Wallace (eds.)
    1996   *Policy-Making in the European Union* (Oxford: Oxford University Press, 3rd edn).

Wallace, William
    1983   'Less than a Federation, More than a Regime: The Community as Political System', in Helen Wallace, William Wallace and Carole Webb (eds.), *Policy Making in the European Community* (Chichester: John Wiley): 403-36.
    1991   'Foreign Policy and National Identity in the United Kingdom', *International Affairs* 67.1: 65-70.
    1994   *Regional Integration: The West European Experience* (Washington, DC: The Brookings Institution).
    1996   'Government without Statehood: The Unstable Equilibrium', in Wallace and Wallace (eds.) 1996: 439-60.

Wallace, William, and Julie Smith
    1995   'Democracy versus Technocracy, European Integration and the Problem of Popular Consent', *West European Politics* 18.3: 137-57.

Weiler, Joseph H.H.
    1992   'After Maastricht: Community Legitimacy in Post-1992 Europe', in William James Adams (ed.), *Singular Europe* (Ann Arbor: University of Michigan Press): 11-41.

Welle, Klaus
    1998   Secretary General of the European People's Party, Interview with the author, 3 December.

Westlake, Martin
    1994a   *A Modern Guide to the European Parliament* (London: Pinter).
    1994b   *The Commission and the Parliament: Partners and Rivals in the European Policy-making Process* (London: Butterworths).
    1994c   *Britain's Emerging Euro-Elite? The British in the Directly-Elected European Parliament, 1979–1992* (Aldershot: Dartmouth Publishing Company Limited).

1997   '"Mad Cows and Englishmen": The Institutional Consequences of the
           BSE Crisis', *Journal of Common Market Studies* 35.Annual Review: 11-
           36.
1998   'The European Parliament's Emerging Powers of Appointment', *Journal
           of Common Market Studies* 36.3: 431-44.
Wheare, K.C.
1963   *Legislatures* (New York: Oxford University Press).

GENERAL INDEX

INDEX OF AUTHORS